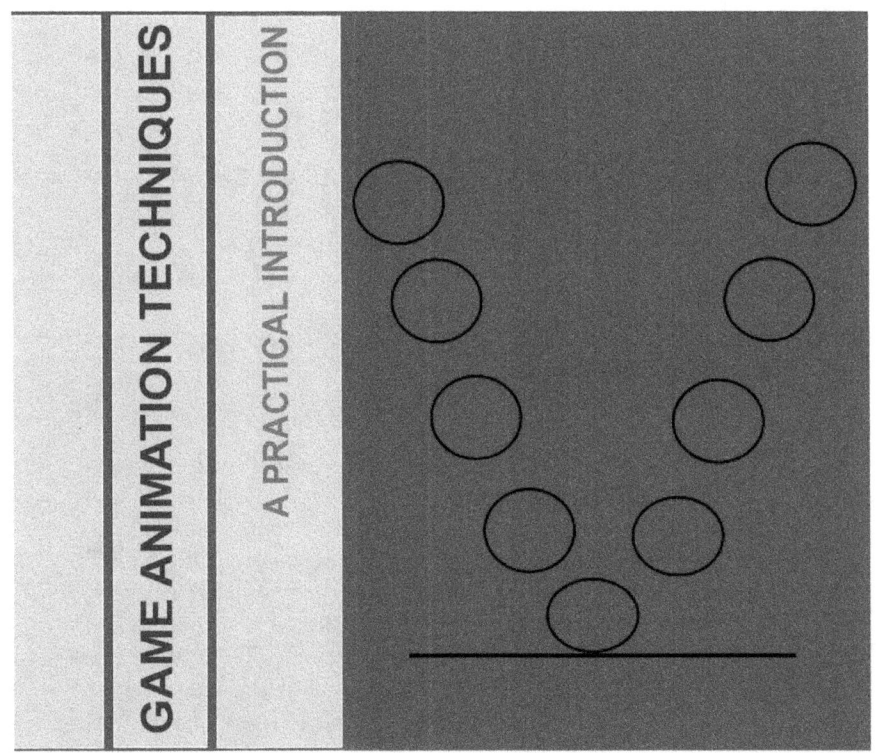

Game Animation Techniques An introduction to animation techniques for
A Practical Introduction real-time gaming environments using practi-
Kenwright cal examples.

BOOK TITLE:
Game Animation Techniques: A Practical Introduction
ISBN-13: 978-1-523-21068-8
ISBN-10: 1-523-21068-0

Edition: 010101016

For information or any other inquiries, please contact:
apracticalintroduction@gmail.com

Table of Contents

Table of Contents

Table of Contents

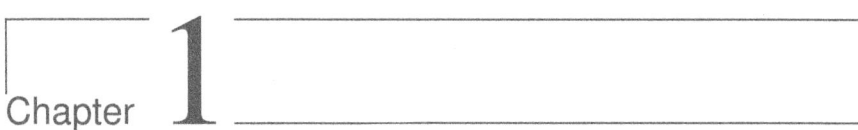

Chapter 1

Introduction and Overview

"We cannot solve our problems with the same thinking we used when we created them."

Albert Einstein

1.1 Introduction

Animation or 'motion' covers a wide range of topics - from simple timing and trigonometric concepts all the way through to calculus and procedural algorithms. The applications are enormous - on-line control of character motions, trajectory design and graphical mechanisms, robotics, and of course animation systems. We explain the theory behind animation principles in addition to implementation details for use in interactive environments, such as, video games and training simulations, including core mathematics (vectors, matrices, cross/dot product, and the plane equation). This textbook is designed to guide the reader in a practical sense to indispensable topic of animation. Organized around the central concept of animation and motion, the book includes numerous real-world examples in the body of the text, while showing limitations and engineering workarounds to common problems. It is also one of the purposes of this book to introduce the reader to the development aspects of video games and real-time interactive software.

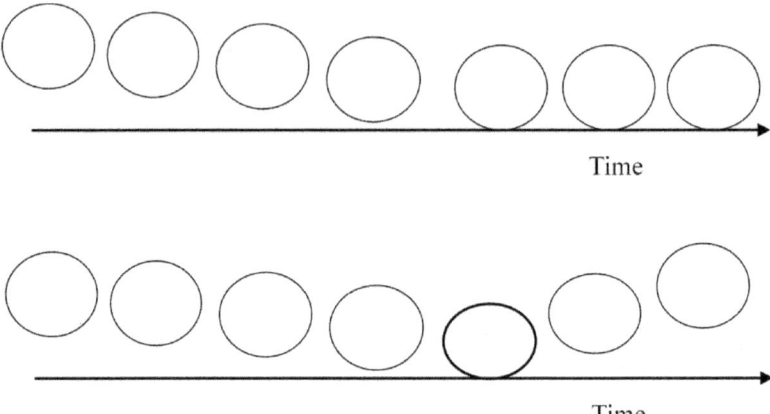

Figure 1.1. *Animation Concept - The principle we are attempting to create, is the 'illusion' of movement. For example, a ball falling in the figure. While we capture the basic translational concept from the starting position to the ground, we also need to think about 'aesthetic' concepts; such as, how the ball 'reacts' when colliding with other objects. Following on, we'll also discuss 'active' and 'passive' animations - such as, animations of dumb objects, like rocks and balls, and active objects, like characters and animations.*

1.2 Games

Have you ever thought about how game animations are done? What secrets and tricks are used to achieve the impossible? As games need to 'appear' incredibly detailed and life-like in addition to running at real-time frame-rates. While games strive for photo-realism, games are also packed with movement. Characters running, bullets flying, dust particles swooshing - basically there is an abundance of action and motion - this brings an otherwise static scene to life. These motions may use a variety of techniques. A common property, is the motions must remain coherent and smooth - this is an important detail that can often break the illusion of realism and is often overlooked. However, this is only one of the many challenges we need to address - while allowing artists and developers the freedom and creativity they require to meet the next generation of game technologies. In fact, we need to understand not only the mechanics behind the motion in general, but how time and motion are connected. For example, a whole range of objects are moving in a game, from cameras and characters to particles and sky-domes. We explain each of these concepts step-by-step throughout the following chapters - starting with basic principles, such as, geometric blending, all the way through to more procedural methods, like physics-based techniques (springs and ragdolls).

1.3 What are Animations?

While animations are technically movement (or changing state), there are a number of other factors we need to consider - such as, the level of detail, resolution, life-like qualities, squash and stretch - all these factors and more fall under animation techniques. In this book, we are interested in real-time solutions that produce aesthetically pleasing results - an animation does not necessary have to look or move realistically - we may be interested in artistic qualities. We explain how the digital world is changing and how animations are achieved in interactive environments - how pre-recorded animations can be combine with physics-based and procedural techniques to captivate and immerse the user.

1.4 What is hard about Animations?

Creating a scene full of movement is challenging and important. We can't just record every piece of movement in a scene and play it back - it would produce a static repetitive scene - furthermore, it would be too expensive to store and modify. We need to use a number of different techniques to create the illusion of detail. For example, a sky full of clouds, leaves falling from trees, car exhaust smoke, rain drops, animated characters, flags flapping in the wind - each of these animation effects uses a different technique. This enables us to simulate a virtual world full of life and movement in real-time that is interactive.

1.5 Theory & Practice

Each chapter focuses on a specific area of animation - explaining the theory in addition to providing simplified code listings and implementation examples (Figure 1.2). Each chapter aims to help the reader understand a specific topic - from the ground up - that is - both the theory behind the equations and technique and its application and implementation. Applying the theory is important to understanding. The reader should build upon a minimalistic sample - both dissecting and experimenting to solidify their comprehension of the topic - enabling them to embellish and combine solutions that go above and beyond to meet cutting edge demands of tomorrow.

1.6 Artistic Qualities (Stretch, Collision, and Blur)

As shown in Figure 1.1, even the simplest animation, such as, a ball bouncing, requires secondary features to emphasis realism, like squash, acceleration, and collision response. A simple ball bouncing can be achieved using a basic particle system as explained in Chapter 6 - using mass, velocity, and springs (with a point mass representing the centre of the sphere). However, the motion may be 'physically' correct but appear lacking - we can improve this by adding extra artistic details. This can be as simple as stretching the object along the velocity direction and echoing the object's trajectory at high speeds to show motion effects. Mixing in both artistic control and secondary procedural effects requires more work but makes the final motion more captivating and realistic.

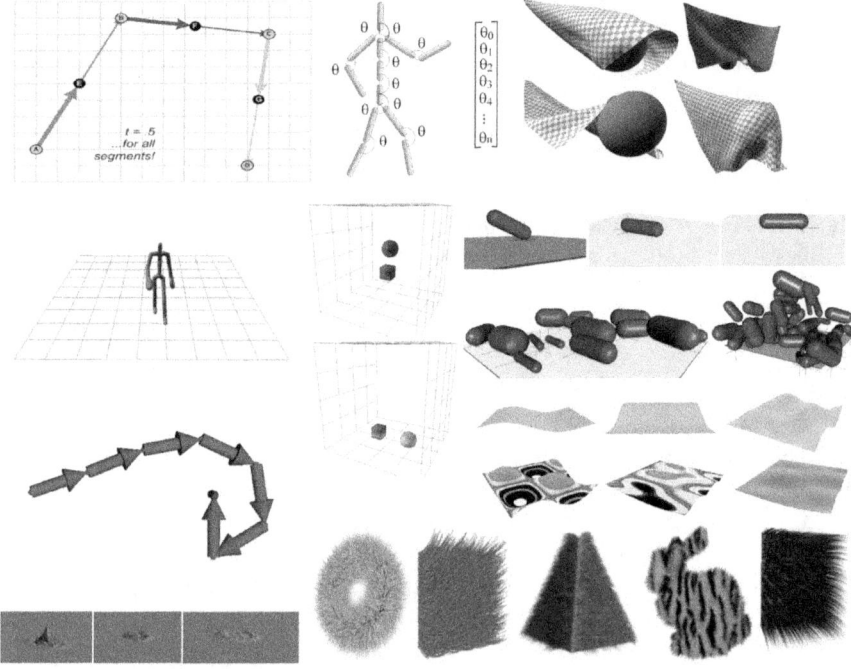

Figure 1.2. *Chapter Samples - Demonstrate the different animation techniques using simplified examples that the reader can expand upon.*

1.7 Summary

This book aims to introduce the concept of animation techniques related to real-time environments, such as, video games. It is recommended that the reader also review literature and material to supplement their knowledge and understanding of the subject. For example, there are a variety of books on mathematics, graphical techniques, classical mechanics and physics-based simulators that would complement this text. It is important for beginners to understand the application of animation principles in different areas of interactive technologies (e.g., video games, training simulators, and computer animation). The classical concepts from trigonometry, calculus (rate of change), and kinematics define generalized rules, such as, positions, velocities, and accelerations - which are used to build equations and create mathematical models that show animation techniques in action (the foundation of creating motion). Each chapter concentrates on a single animation technique; aside from the first few informational chapters (core mathematical and programming concepts), the book is completely modular, meaning you can skip the chapters you are not interest in and get right to the topics that you're looking to learn more about.

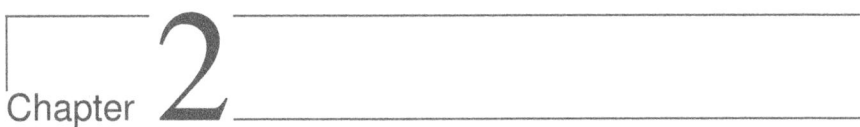

Chapter **2**

Programming

No great mind has ever existed without a touch of madness.

Aristotle

2.1 Introduction

When you implementing a solution in code you should have no error of doubt
about what your code does. There should be no magic, luck, or guesswork
involved. You should aim to write fast, reliable, readable code. Furthermore, it should work every time (e.g., not 99% of the time) and when some
unavoidable set of circumstances does happen (e.g., a typing error or from
bad input data) your code should be able to identifying where, when and
how the problem occurred. Your code should never crash with a bug that
leaves you, or anyone else, standing in the dark guessing and wondering why
or how it happened and how on earth you can fix it. This section discusses
good coding ethics, tactics, pitfalls, and hints on what to look out for when
implementing your collision detection algorithms.

Anyhow, less ranting! You might skip this chapter and jump straight into
the animation techniques. However, you'll find that experience and pain will
eventually lead you back here. Remember, to always keep the code readable
and simple then you should *mostly* be okay.

2.2 Which Programming Language? (C++, C#, Java, or Fortran)

You might ask: Which is the best programming language? Which is the fastest? Which is the most portable? Which is the most used? Every programming language has different advantages and disadvantages. While the *majority* of code in this book is based on C++ it should be relatively straightforward to port it to different programming languages is necessary.

This is an introductory text with an emphasis on simplicity, practicality, and clarity using stripped-down examples. Hence, the implementations have not been optimized for speed. Once the reader fully grasps the principle, he/she is free to rewrite and improve the different solutions. In the majority of cases, the demos will run in real-time at 30 or more frames per second (fps); however, with any interactive environment, such as games, it can never be fast enough.

2.3 Asserts

The "assert" statement is a programmer's best friend. It's your friend. It won't slow your code down. It won't make your code less readable. It will help you catch errors and make your code more reliable and robust. In summary, asserts will help you write better code, so use them!

2.3.1 Where should you place your Asserts?

A logical place to put the majority of your asserts is at the beginning of your functions. Since it is smart to ensure all the parameters being passed to your functions are valid and within acceptable tolerances. For example, in the majority of cases you'll require that your quaternion functions to operate with *unit-quaternions*. Hence, you should check that the quaternions you are working with are of length one, otherwise assert and give a warning.

If you do identify a problem with an assert. For example, the value being passed in is invalid. Don't try to engineer a function by incorporating hacks or workarounds so that the program works without complaining. The hack will only come back and bite you later. If you do integrate in a *temporary* fix ensure you do it for only yourself and leave the assert warning in place.

2.3.2 Difference between a 'System' Assert and a 'Custom' Assert

Don't use the system assert. Define your own custom assert so you have full control over what happens when an assert is triggered. It enables you to easily enable/disable/modify the logic for an assert for different builds. For example, in a final build of your application you may prefer that asserts log errors to a debug file and continue to run. However, in debug you want the assert to trigger a breakpoint and stop on the aforementioned line to enable you to fix the problem.

```
1
2  #ifdef _DEBUG
3
4  //#define DBG_HALT __asm{ int 3 } // or __debugbreak();
5
6    #define DBG_HALT { __debugbreak(); } // visual studio debugger ←
         halt
7    #define DBG_ASSERT(exp) {if ( !(exp) ) {DBG_HALT;}}
8    #define DBG_CHECKFLOAT(f) \
9    {
10     DBG_ASSERT( f!=f ); // NAN (not-a-number)
11     DBG_ASSERT( f!=infinity );
12     DBG_ASSERT( f!=-infinity );
13   }
14 #else
15   #define DBG_HALT
16   #define DBG_ASSERT(exp)
17   #define DBG_CHECKFLOAT(f)
18 #endif // _DEBUG
19
20
21 // Optional other sanity checks
22
23 #define DBG_CHECKVECTOR3(v) \
24 {
25   DBG_CHECKFLOAT( v.x );
26   DBG_CHECKFLOAT( v.y );
27   DBG_CHECKFLOAT( v.z );
28 }
29
30 #define DBG_QUATERNION(q) \
31 {
32   DBG_CHECKFLOAT( q.x );
33   DBG_CHECKFLOAT( q.y );
34   DBG_CHECKFLOAT( q.z );
35   DBG_CHECKFLOAT( q.w );
36 }
```

Listing 2.1. Custom Debug Asserts

2.4 Numbers

What is a number? Why do we use floats instead of doubles? What happens when we try to convert a float into an integer? For example, what is 0.68f as an integer? If you don't know then it might be time to pull out that thick programming book holding up your desk.

You should be well aware of the three primary numbers you'll encounter during coding and are defined as:

- floats
- doubles
- integers

(let's keep it simple and focus on 32-bit signed integers - we don't want to open the box of unsigned/signed, shorts, bytes and so forth - I also hope nobody thinks a 'short int' has anything to do with clothing or short legged trousers). Some people in this world think that a byte and a nibble have something to do with food! However, you must always be aware of approximation errors, rounding problems, acceptable ranges, and invalid operations (e.g., divide by zero). While the majority of the time you can incorporate corrective measures to handle numerical inaccuracies you must always be on your guard. Never assume or guess otherwise it will only come back and bite you later.

2.5 Radians or Degrees

The answer is simple - always use radians. Radians are your friend! Radians are a rational mathematical quantity. Radians are the natural unit for trigonometric functions, with a full circle of rotation given by 2π radians.

While radians and degrees, of course, are both arbitrary ways of measuring angles, radians are, in general, more convenient for, say, calculus and geometric applications, because they play nicer with other functions that are useful (e.g., sine, cosine, and dot-product). Hence, we always assume angular values are in radians unless otherwise specified.

2.6 Angular Issues (0, 2π, 4π, ...)

The circular nature of angles means that two angles can represent the same angle. For example, $\frac{\pi}{2}$ is the same as $-\frac{\pi}{2}$ and 0 is the same as 2π, 4π, 6π, and so on. This can complicate things when we have limits and ranges. Keep this in mind for later on when we work with systems with multiple angular joints (e.g., in a human character model). Typically, when we work with angular displacements, always ensure the angular change is relatively small to keep the system stable and avoid jumping across multiple angular circumferences (e.g., it can bring the system crashing down if random chaotic angles being used as a solution to the animation problem).

2.6.1 Fixed Angular Range

We ensure our angles always remain within the range 0 to 2π (e.g., angular deviations of 10 or 100 would result in non-continuous random jumps).

Sporadic angular spikes can be the result of unsolvable solutions that have converged on unrealistic and impractical solutions.

One possible solution is to take smaller steps between iterations to see if this resolves the problem. Alternatively, if you are solving the problem globally using a matrix inversion you could increase the damping constant.

2.7 Repeating Code

As a rule, you should never repeat code, if you can avoid it. However, there are special cases, for example, your debug code or a temporary algorithm you're working on at that moment. Nevertheless, as a general rule, don't!

One of the biggest, "kick in the teeth", that people can come across is the dreaded "copy and paste" mistake! You copy a chunk of code from another place and rename or rewrite the variables or blocks of code that you can see. However, you can miss one or two tiny variables and still have it work. It's only days or weeks down the line when you start getting strange bugs or problems. In short, make sure you include lots of sanity checks and run your code thought as many test cases as you can, so it's solid and robust.

2.8 Arrays

Don't fall into the trap of going outside array boundaries. For example, the problems of memory corruption and random values can be difficult to track down in un-managed memory implementations (i.e., in C or C++). For an example see Listing 2.2.

```
1    int vals[4];
2    vals[4] = 2; // Will corrupt memory without any warning
3
4    // Array is a template wrapper class
```

```
5    Array<int> vals[4];
6    vals[4] = 2; // Will assert and tell you array bounds exceeded
```

Listing 2.2. Array (C++) - which is better and why?

It should be noted, however, that for managed C# examples, this can be less of a problem, since array lengths and boundaries checks are incorporated by default into the language.

2.9 Generally

It's easy to get into bad coding habits, than into good ones. You'll tell yourself that you will never make that mistake, or you understand why you did it that why. Then again, have you ever looked at another person's code and thought it was rubbish, untidy, unclear? Don't let that other person's code be yours.

For example, look at the following sample code in Listing 2.3 and decide which is better and why?

```
1   if ( 2==x )
2   {
3       // something
4   }
5
6   if ( x==2 )
7   {
8       // something
9   }
```

Listing 2.3. Example coding style preference - which is better and why?

For those people who can't see the difference between the code snippets in Listing 2.3 the difference is '2==x' and 'x==2' inside the if statement.

The code logic in its current state would compile and run without a problem on $C/C\#/C++/Java$ without any difficulty. However, the problem occurs when we mistype code (since nobody's perfect). When we accidently do 'x=2' instead of 'x==2', what will happen? In some languages like $C/C++$ it will compile merrily without complaining. How can it know if we meant to do 'x=2' or 'x==2'? Since some people write code like this intentionally, and believe a single line statement is superior. Therefore, a typing mistake can go unnoticed in code causing problems later down the line.

Then again, in $C\#$ and Java the compiler will give an error if we attempt to do 'x=2' since it requires a boolean value (i.e., if x isn't a boolean).

My advice is, if it makes your code less ambiguous, clear and error prone then why not use it. For old-school programmers it can be difficult to break the mold (i.e., habit) since the majority of text books have taught us that 'x==2' is acceptable. On the other hand, don't be a sheep and do things because someone else did with no logical reason. Always question the reason and logic, and ask if there is a better, faster, more reliable approach.

```
1
2   if ( x!=x )
3   {
4   // something
5   }
6
7   if ( x=!x )
8   {
9   // something
10  }
```

Listing 2.4. Warnings - make sure you understand a warning and make sure you don't mistype code - both of these lines compile, but what is the difference? (a clue is NANs).

For Listing 2.4, 'x!=x', you would obviously expect the variable to always equal itself? However, when a mathematical error has occurred and we get a 'NAN' - this operation will fail. The advantage of this is, it's a common test on multiple languages, such as, C++ and Java. The operation 'x=!x' will invert the variable and overwrite the current value.

2.10 Fast or Reliable

The majority of the time you are more interested in code that doesn't take a week to simulate. In interactive environments, such as games, speed is everything. However, don't be sloppy. Don't write code that is fast but only works one in three times. I would say write clear, well-defined, reliable code to begin with - then and only then worry about speed.

2.11 'My' Function - Wrappers

As you become more experienced and your game engine or collision detection library grows you'll eventually start to wrap common functions, such as cos, sin, sqrt, within a set of wrappers (e.g., mycos, mysin, mysqrt). The first thing you might ask, is why? Why would you want to do that when cos, sin, sqrt are all common math functions? The reason is, we can validate values and trap errors at the point they occur. If an invalid number is passed into any of our wrapper functions, we can assert and halt when it happens and quickly track down who or what caused it. As shown in Listing 2.5, we assert if a 'NAN' or out of bounds number is passed in as a parameter to our function.

```
1  float mycos( float val )
2  {
3    DBG_CHECKFLOAT( val );
4    DBG_ASSERT( val>=-1 && val <=1 );
5    return cos( val )
6  };
```

Listing 2.5. 'My' Wrapper Function Example

2.12 Traps and Pitfalls

Some common bugs:

- Avoid division by zero - we need to be sure the divider is never zero even with possible floating point errors
- Avoid square root of a negative number - when repairing a pure rotation matrix we need to be sure that the tr value chosen is never negative even with possible floating point errors or de-orthogonalised matrix input
- Accuracy of dividing by (and square rooting) a very small number - with floating point numbers, dividing small numbers by small numbers should be reasonably accurate but at the extreme it would loose accuracy
- Resiliency for a de-orthogonalised matrix (i.e., numerical errors, approximations, and drifting can create erroneous distorted matrices)

2.13 Summary

Don't get stressed! Don't burn out on late night programming sessions with coffee as a replacement for food. Don't guess! Don't leave hacks and bodges in final versions of the code, which you tell yourself you'll come back and fix one day. Comments are good for code. Try and avoid naming all the variables with abstract names, such as, a, b, c, e, f, g, and j.

Chapter 3

Core Concepts

Life is like a box of chocolates; you never know what you're going to get.

Forest Gump

3.1 Introduction

This chapter introduces a number of core concepts common in animation techniques. We explain a number of fundamental techniques common in a many animations - setting the ground work for later more advanced concepts that build upon these simple ideas (e.g., timing and interpolation). Most time based animations are evolve around an object moving a distance over a period of time. We explain how to correlate the movement and time - so they correspond with the real-world. Understanding the difference between continuous and discrete systems - and acceptable resolutions. At the end of this chapter, you should be able to interpolate objects along paths in addition to animating data using key-frame structures. We'll show you how to point an objects in the direction it's travelling - using the forward vector and the target direction vector. We calculate the change in angle necessary to orient our mesh so it points in the desired direction. Interpolation isn't just used for position - it is used in a whole range of exciting subjects - from cinematic effect (changing field of view and camera orientation) all the way through to sound modulation and blending.

3.2 Trigonometry

You need to remember your basic trigonometry from high-school. For example, Pythagoras theorem and trigonometry functions, such as, cosine, sine, and tangent.

For instance, the ability to convert from $cos(\theta)$ to $sin(\theta)$ - i.e., using:

$$sin(\theta) = sin(acos(cos(\theta)))$$

or (3.1)

$$sin(\theta) = \sqrt{(1 - cos(\theta))}$$

If you're a bit rusty on these concepts, like the cosine rule, you need to dig out that old maths book and brush up, otherwise, some of the techniques we discuss will just go right over your head.

3.3 Timing

3.3.1 Virtual Clock

Timing information is central to any animation system. We are able to increment or decrement time of a system - the 'virtual clock' so to say. As in the real-world - we have 'time' and 'seconds'. We should be familiar with this concept, as we it in our daily lives. However, unlike in the 'real-world' - we are unable to alter time. For example, speed it up or even make it travel backwards.

3.3.2 Discrete Time

Computers are 'discrete' systems. Time is incremented by specific amounts. We need to be aware of what 'discrete' means. For example, if the time increment (i.e., the 'time step'), is too large, we'll notice artefacts and the motion will be jumpy, unnatural, and non-smooth. While if we make the time step too small, it can use a large amount of system resources, such as, computational time and system memory.

- milli-seconds $\frac{1}{100}$ second
- minutes 60 seconds

- hours   60 minutes (or $60 \times 60 seconds$)
- micro-seconds $\frac{1}{1000000}$ second

$$\text{frame rate} = \text{frames per second (fps)} = \frac{1}{\text{iterations}} \qquad (3.2)$$

- Cinema   - 24 fps
- Television (UK)   - 26 fps
- Television (USA)   - 24 fps
- Physics Simulator   - 30+ fps

3.3.3 Fixed & Variable Frame Rates

Depending upon the situation and the data - the frame rate may be 'variable'. For example, a ball travelling in a straight line, only needs the start and end locations. Knowing the start time, we are then able to calculate the position of the ball at any moment in time between those two points. However, we must be aware of 'visual' factors - if the animation has a graphical output or if the object is 'interacting' with the scene or other objects. As the time step increases, the visual animation will start to 'jump' from frame to frame - rather than smoothly transitioning.

3.4 Compression

The first reason to use compression is to reduce the file size of animations (e.g., physical foot-print on your hard-drive).

Two main types of compression are:

- lossy compression - the original data isn't the same as the decompressed data (i.e., loss in information to reduce the size)
- lossless compression - the compress data contains the exact same information as the original data

Whole range of compression algorithms, some that are more generic (e.g., run-length encoding or file compression (zip)). A particular animation compression is to remove redundancy by disposing of repeating frame (known as frame disposal). The frame disposal method specifies whether a user would like to discard a current frame before the next frame is displayed. To reduce the size of the animation a user should discard a current frame and then work on the next. However they must make sure that they are happy with the frame as they will be unable to recover the frame once is has been discarded. This technique reduces the size of the animations because there are less frames in an animation.

The technique of frame disposal can be expanded to include specific components of an animation - such as, individual joint animations. As full body character animations use arrays of angular joint changes. Rather than saving a whole body list of joint changes, only the joints that change frame-by-frame are needed (reduce degrees of freedom).

For example:

- Bitwise Compression (i.e., raw binary - not take into account the data - generic)
- Remove Every Second Key
- Remove Linear Keys
- Compress Each Track Independently
- Remove Trivial Keys
- Revert To Raw (i.e., strip out any complex animation information, splines, non-linear interpolation, to 'raw' frame-by-frame data)

3.5 Fidelity (Resolution)

As objects move faster, we require a faster and faster frame rate to capture the necessary details. This is due to the fact that computers are 'discrete' systems - and capture slices of the data. If the slices are too far apart, then the play-back will lack fidelity - appearing jerky and non-smooth. While televisions refresh at 25-30 frames per second (fps) - for animations, we need to sample much higher (60+ fps).

Highly dynamic animations (faster frame-rate)   For fast paced animations, such as, car crashes, jumping and punching, it may be necessary to sample at a much faster frame-rate to ensure the recordings capture enough details.

3.6 Level of detail (animation)

The amount of data required to reproduce the scene is a rough approximation of level of detail (LOD).

3.7 Interpolation

3.7.1 Linear (LERP)

$$(1 - t)v0 + tv1 \tag{3.3}$$

```
1    // Imprecise method which does not guarantee v = v1 when t = 1,
2    // due to floating-point arithmetic error.
3    float lerp(float v0, float v1, float t)
4    {
5        return v0 + t*(v1-v0);
6    }
7
8    // Precise method which guarantees v = v1 when t = 1.
9    float lerp(float v0, float v1, float t)
10   {
11       return (1-t)*v0 + t*v1;
12   }
13
```

3.7.2 Fast In/Fast Out

One way to move slower at the start and faster towards the end would be to
square the time:

```
1  vector currentPos = posA  + (posB - posA) * (timeValue * timeValue);
```

While the graph for a linear transition is a straight line - for the square time,
we would get a parabola. To move faster at the start and slower at the end:

```
1  float t = 1 - timeValue;
2  vector currentPos = posA  + (posB - posA) * t * t;
```

3.7.3 Angular

What is special about angular interpolation (e.g., π and 2π)?

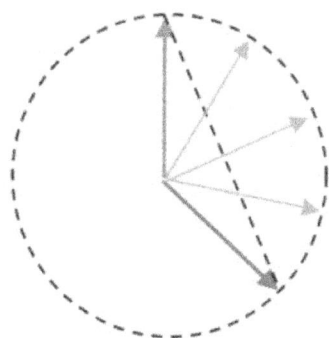

Figure 3.1. *Angular Interpolation* - *Subdividing the line and not the arc.*

Small Angles

For small angles, we are able to use a linear interpolation.

$$P(t) = A + (B - A)t \tag{3.4}$$

Or more accurately, $\text{Slerp}(p_0, p_1; t) = (1 - t)p_0 + tp_1..$

Normalized LERP (NLERP)

As shown in Figure 3.1, we linearly interpolate between the two control points, but apply an additional normalization stage to ensure the point is projected onto the arc.

Large Angles

We now address the following questions: How do we represent orientation/-transforms? What problems do we have with interpolating this? How to identify the shortest path and axis in 3D Why do we use quaternions?

Quaternion Interpolation

As with complex numbers:

Lerp:

$$q(t) = (1 - t)q_0 + tq_1 \tag{3.5}$$

Slerp

$$q(t) = \frac{sin(1 - t)\alpha}{sin\alpha}q_0 + \frac{sint\alpha}{sin\alpha}q_1 \tag{3.6}$$

where q_0 is the first quaternion (from), q_1 is the second quaternion (to), $q(t)$ is the interpolated quaternion, t is a scalar between 0 and 1, α is the half angle between q_0 and q_1.

The interpolation technique depends upon the data. For example, Lerp is generally good enough for most situations. Slerp is generally used mostly in graphics (i.e., other than camera/motion control). We also must ensure we, normalize quaternion (i.e., keep a unit-quaternion).

```
1
2    Quaternion Slerp(const Quaternion& qa,
3                     const Quaternion& qb,
4                     double t)
5    {
6        // quaternion to return
7        Quaternion qm = Quaternion::Identity();
8
9        // Calculate angle between them.
10       double cosHalfTheta = qa.w * qb.w + qa.x * qb.x + qa.y * qb.y ↩
     + qa.z * qb.z;
11
12       // if qa=qb or qa=-qb then theta = 0 and we can return qa
13       if (abs(cosHalfTheta) >= 1.0)
14       {
15           qm.w = qa.w;qm.x = qa.x;qm.y = qa.y;qm.z = qa.z;
16           return qm;
17       }
18
19       // Calculate temporary values.
20       double halfTheta = acos(cosHalfTheta);
21       double sinHalfTheta = sqrt(1.0 - cosHalfTheta*cosHalfTheta);
22
23       // if theta = pi radians then result is not fully defined
24       // we could rotate around any axis normal to qa or qb
25       if (fabs(sinHalfTheta) < 0.001){ // fabs is floating point ↩
     absolute
26           qm.w = (qa.w * 0.5 + qb.w * 0.5);
27           qm.x = (qa.x * 0.5 + qb.x * 0.5);
28           qm.y = (qa.y * 0.5 + qb.y * 0.5);
29           qm.z = (qa.z * 0.5 + qb.z * 0.5);
30           return qm;
31       }
32       double ratioA = sin((1 - t) * halfTheta) / sinHalfTheta;
33       double ratioB = sin(t * halfTheta) / sinHalfTheta;
34
35       //calculate Quaternion.
36       qm.w = (qa.w * ratioA + qb.w * ratioB);
37       qm.x = (qa.x * ratioA + qb.x * ratioB);
38       qm.y = (qa.y * ratioA + qb.y * ratioB);
39       qm.z = (qa.z * ratioA + qb.z * ratioB);
40       return qm;
41   }// End Slerp(..)
42
```

Listing 3.1. When theta is π radians, the result is undefined because there is no shortest direction to rotate - one option is to choose some arbitrary axis that is normal to qa or qb (see Equation 3.6).

3.8 Paths/Splines

Paths and splines allows you to traverse smoothly through a set of defined points (in some cases, tangents too). Mathematically, it is defined as $P(t)$ where t is $[0, 1]$, where 0 is the start of the path/spline, and 1 is the end of the path.

3.8.1 Bezier

To understand how the Bezier spline concept works, we consider increasingly complex situations - that is, linear, quadratic, and cubic problem.

Linear Bezier (Two Points)

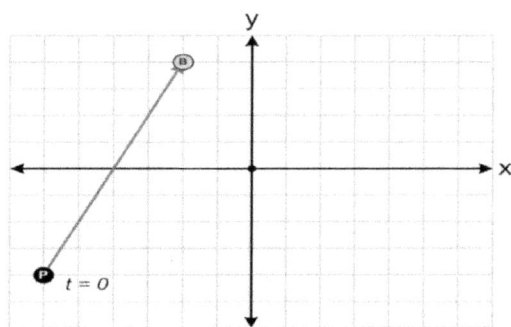

Figure 3.2. *Linear Bezier - Linear Bezier problem is analogous to the linear interpolation between two control points A and B.*

The linear Bezier problem, has two control points A and B and a ratio t (0 to 1).

$$P = (A(1 - t) + B(t))$$

$$\text{or} \tag{3.7}$$

$$P = As + Bt$$

where $s = 1 - t$, A and B are the control points, while t is a scalar from 0 to 1;

Quadratic Bezier (Three Points)

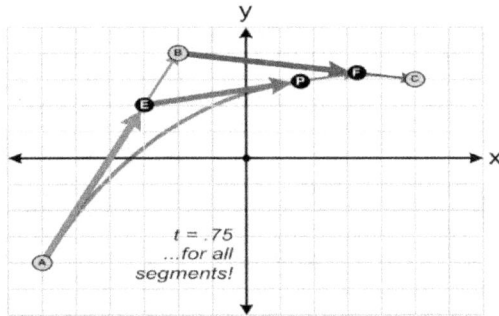

Figure 3.3. ***Quadratic Bezier*** *- Three three control points ABC are divided into two linear Bezier problems AB and AC.*

Represent the problem as a combination of two linear Bezier curves (AB and BC).

$$
\begin{aligned}
E(t) &= sA + tB \qquad (remember, s = 1 - t)\\
F(t) &= sB + tC \qquad\qquad\qquad\qquad\qquad (3.8)\\
P(t) &= sE + tF
\end{aligned}
$$

Substitute and re-arrange the problem, we get Equation 3.9 below:

$$
\begin{aligned}
P(t) &= sE(t) + tF(t)\\
&= s(sA + tB) + t(sB + tC)\\
&= (s^2)A + (st)B + (st)B + (t^2)C \qquad (3.9)\\
&= (s^2)A + 2(st)B + (t^2)C
\end{aligned}
$$

Note the 'squared' quadratic component - t^2. Importantly, the quadratic Bezier curve is just a blend of two linear Bezier curves, so the mathematics is simple to understand and derive. Typically, you'll use quadratic Bezier for smooth corners (e.g., True Type Fonts are infinity smooth and curvy due this technique).

Cubic Bezier (Four Points)

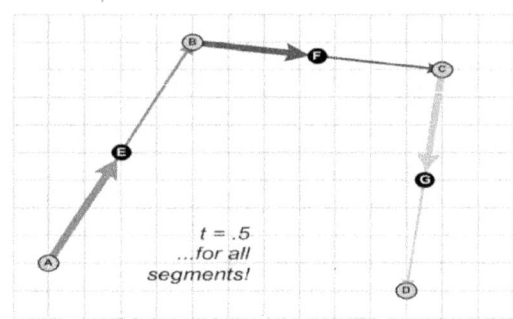

Figure 3.4. *Cubic Bezier* - *Four control points ABCD are divided into multiple linear Bezier problems.*

$$E(t) = sA + tB$$
$$F(t) = sB + tC \qquad (3.10)$$
$$G(t) = sC + tD$$

Combining and re-arranging so we have a single equation:

$$P(t) = (s^3)A + 3(s^2t)B + 3(st^2)C + (t^3)D \qquad (3.11)$$

Note our cubic value, i.e., t^3

3.8.2 Catmull-Rom Spline

The Catmull-Rom spline Equation 3.12 for two control points is given below and possesses the following key characteristics that are desirable for controlled trajectories.

$$\begin{aligned} q(t) = 0.5 \big(\ &(2P_1)+ \\ &(-P_0 + P_2)t+ \\ &(2P_0 - 5P_1 + 4P_2 - P_3)t^2+ \\ &(-P_0 + 3P_1 - 3P_2 + P_3)t^3 \ \big) \end{aligned} \qquad (3.12)$$

- The spline **passes through all of the control points**
- The spline is continuous (i.e., first derivative), meaning that there are **no discontinuities** in the tangent direction and magnitude

- The spline is not continuous for the second derivative, however, linearly interpolating each segment, causes the curvature to vary linearly over the length of the segment
- Points on a segment may lie outside of the domain

The most crucial feature of the Catmull-Rom spline worth noting, is the specified curve 'passes through all of the control points' (e.g., this is not true of all types of splines, such as, Bezier spline).

3.8.3 Spline Caching

We cache the result of splines at loading time, using the pre-loaded data set, The splines are calculated using the stored points. So you only need to evaluate the splines once. *Trading memory for CPU time.* This is especially important for static meshes/scenes.

3.9 Following a Path

When we have an object on the z-plane - we typically want it to rotate in the direction it is travelling. The simplest solution is to use the 'dot' and 'cross' product to calculate the axis and angle to rotate the object in the correct direction (Figure 3.5). In addition, once we can work out the current and desired direction - we can 'interpolate' the change in direction to produce a smooth and visually pleasing result (i.e., avoid abrupt 'snapping' when changing direction). The two methods for interpolating the change in direction - are either increment the angle (axis-angle into a matrix transform) - or create a quaternion from the axis-angle and use SLERP to interpolate (assuming the current orientation is in a quaternion).

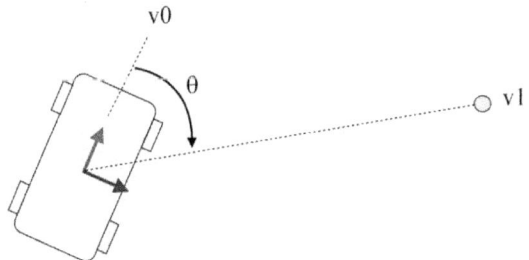

Figure 3.5. *Axis-Angle Forward* - *Face the object in the direction we are travelling,* $\theta = acos(v0 \cdot v1)$, *and* $axis = v0 \times v1$.

3.10 Time and Distance

Assuming we are measuring time in seconds, with the distance stored as scalar float. Currently, we have used an arbitrary scalar value from 0 to 1 with no relation to change in time. So what is the time from the start to the current location? If we are sampling the coordinates stored as time, we can compute a value that is time correct, using the following calculation:

$$\text{delta} = \frac{\text{totalTime}}{\text{totalDistance}} \quad (3.13)$$

where totalTime is the total time in seconds from the start to the end of the interpolation, totalDistance is the distance along the trajectory, and delta is a scalar interpolation value (0 to 1).

We use the delta scalar in the computation of the interpolation value.

3.11 Noise

Adding noise improve realism. Organic motion contains a small amount of 'rhythmic' noise on-top of the primary signals. However, the noise needs to be 'coherent' - that is, we can't just add in random changes - it would make the final motion appear to jump - causing sporadic and abrupt changes. We accomplish this using a 'Perlin' noise function.

3.12 Summary

At the end of this chapter, you should have a feel for the essential factors that govern the principle of animation and change. In later chapters, we'll build upon these concepts and introduce more advanced models - applying them to real-world applications.

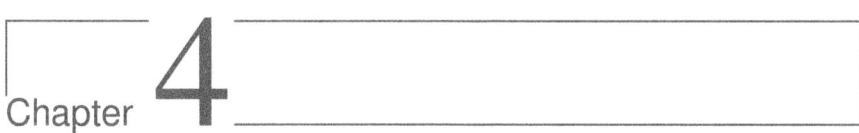

Chapter 4

Geometric

Progress is made by trial and failure; the failures are generally a hundred times more numerous than the successes; yet they are usually left unchronicled.

William Ramsay

4.1 Introduction

Geometric methods form the foundation of most techniques in traditional animation. Interpolating changes with respect to position and rotation with time. The animation data can be procedural or data driven. High level changes to the geometry (i.e., position and rotation) and changes to the geometry's low level properties (i.e., vertex locations and colours). We build upon the concepts introduced in the previous chapter, and apply them to practical examples, for instance, key-frame animations and smooth camera interpolation.

- Key-Frame Animations (Vertex Data)
- Morphing (Blending)
- Vertex/Blending (e.g., MD2)
- Facial Animation

4.2 High Level Object Control

A graphical mesh can be many thousands or hundreds of thousands of vertices. We offload the visual rendering to the graphical processing unit (GPU) - which is well suited to transforming and rendering massive amounts of data to the screen. However, instead of transforming each vertex, we animate the object at a high level - interpolating the linear and angular object transform. The transform can be passed along to the GPU to do all the brute force work of applying it to every vertex.

4.3 Camera Interpolation (Smooth Spring-Like Motion)

When a player moves his animated character around, he'll expect the camera to follow. However, we don't want to 'lock' the camera to the character's motion using linear interpolation - as it would cause a jittery unnatural solution. Instead, we want a 'spring-like' feel - with the camera speeding up and slowing down proportional to the required distance. We talk about springs and physics-based systems in later Chapters. Yet we want to avoid a 'bouncy' oscillatory feel - so we can use an approximate iterative technique - that gradually moves towards the target each frame by a fraction of the error. Causing the camera to speed up and slow down in a smooth manner.

$$p_{n+1} = (p_{target} - p_n) \, k_n; \; dt \qquad (4.1)$$

where p_{target} is the idea location of the camera (e.g., specified distance from the character), p_n is the current camera location, p_{n+1} is the new camera location for the next frame, dt the time-step (0.01), and k_n is the damping constant (around 10). The camera will move faster towards the target for greater error and slow down for smaller errors. While we talk about interpolating the position, the concept can also be applied to other camera parameters, like the field of view (fov) and orientation.

Interpolated (Tweened) Frames

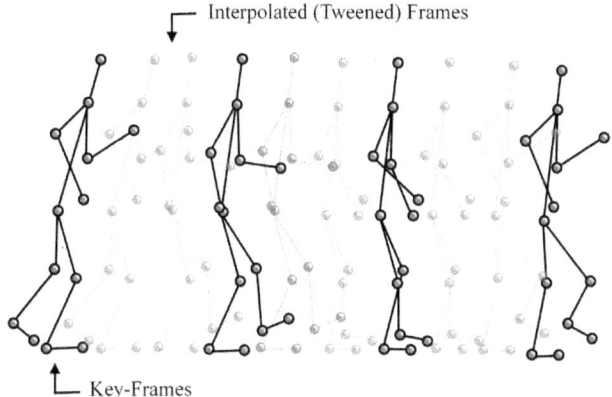

Key-Frames

Figure 4.1. *Key-Frames - Store crucial frames - and the missing inbetween frames are calculated be interpolating between the stored key-frames.*

4.4 Key-Frame Animation

We create 'key-frames' by taking snap shots of the animation pose at specific internals. We then 'interpolate' between the key-frames over time (tweening) - to create the illusion of motion (Figure 4.1). Different data can be stored for each key-frame, such as, individual vertex positions (as shown in the next section with the .md2 format), the joint angles (as described in the next chapter), or physical properties (centre of mass).

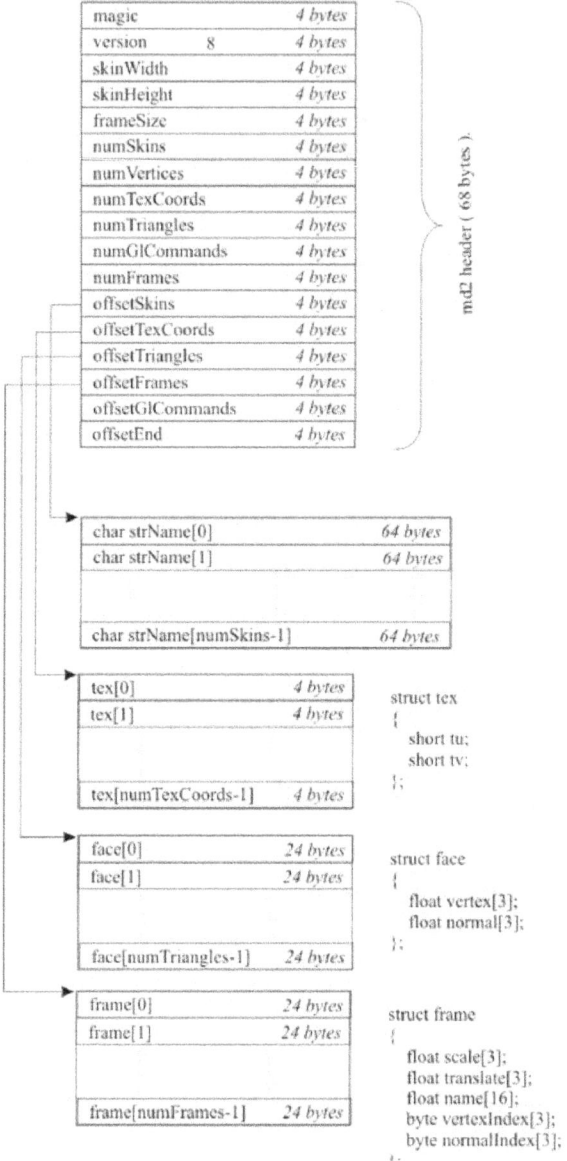

Figure 4.2. Layout MD2 Animation File Format - *The .md2 file format presents a simple example a traditional example of vertex blended character animations.*

4.5 MD2 Format

The .md2 file format is one of the earliest examples of a character animation format using blended vertices (see Figure 4.2). The .md2 format was developed for the video game Quake 2 by ID Software. The good thing of the .md2 file structure is you know up front all the information, such as, offset locations for our 3d file data - i.e., instead of searching through a complex file structure. We review the data within the file format, as shown in Figure 4.2, and explain how to extract and render blended animations.

Numbers:

- numSkins - this simply tells us how many different textures there are, e.g. there could be 3 different bitmap textures that we need to load in.
- numVertices - it tells us how many x,y and z points there are. (note, that it means the total number of unique x,y, z points.... so there would be 60 for example unique x,y,z points reference later in the file format - i.e., when constructing the triangle faces).
- numTexCoords - tells us how many tu, tv coordinates there are.
- numTriangles - each triangle is made up of three sides, this tells us how many triangles (or faces) there are.
- numGlCommands - OpenGL specific, we don't need to know this.
- numFrames - There can be hundreds of frames, this tells us how many there are... e.g. there could be 100 frames, of which we will find out later that 10 maybe for walking, 20 for flying etc.

We should be able to say how much memory we needed now...so we determine our animations memory overhead.

Data Values

All the offset values, e.g. offsetSkins, offsetTriangles etc, is the offset from the start of the file to the actual beginning of the data. So we can jump to the desired location for each data, e.g.,

```
1  fseek( filePointer, offsetSkins, SEEK_SET );
2  fread( pSkins, sizeof(md2Skin), numSkins, filePointer);
```

We need to address the data ordering.

offsetSkins - data is ordered as 64 bytes (e.g. a null terminated string, char md2skin[64];). For example, 'numSkins' indicating the number of skins and also the number of string names (as each skin has a name).

```
1  struct
2  {
3    char strName[64];
4  };
```

offsetTexCoords - an array of 4 bytes, where first 2 bytes is tu, and the next 2 bytes tv. e.g. 2 short integers.

```
1  struct tex
2  {
3    signed short int tu;
4    signed short int tv;
5  };
```

offsetTriangles - each element is 24 bytes, where the first 12 bytes is 3 vertices of 4 bytes each, and the next three 4 bytes are for the normals...I think this can best be seen by doing a quick struct to show how each element would be represented:

```
1  struct face
2  {
3    float vertex[3];
4    float normal[3];
5  };
```

offsetFrames - this is an array of frame values, each frame value is described as follows:

```
1  struct frame
2  {
3    float scale[3];
4    float translate[3];
5    char name[16];
6    byte vertexIndex[3];
7    byte normalIndex[3];
8  };
```

Now that's all there is to the md2 file format, once you get in there and start using it you'll soon see that its really easy to use.

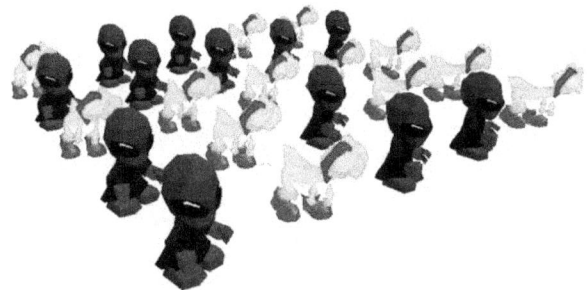

Figure 4.3. *MD2 Loader/Render Screen Capture* - *The md2 file format was originally targeted at low-poly meshes - hence, it is easy to load in lots of animated characters. Since the animation is achieved by interpolating between static key-frame poses - there is very little computational cost.*

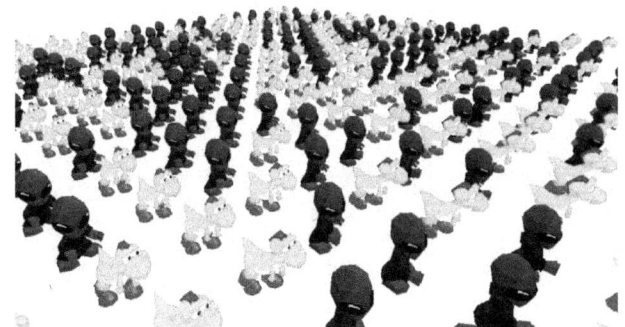

Figure 4.4. *MD2 Loader (Instancing)* - *Without any optimisations - real-time rendering of 625 animated character instances - each having 640 triangle faces.*

4.6 Summary

In any virtual environment, we have geometry (i.e., triangles, meshes, and shapes), both in 2-dimensions and 3-dimensions. How the geometry changes over time in terms of high level details (i.e., overall shape position and rotation) and low level properties (i.e., vertices and colors) allows us to create the illusion of movement (animation).

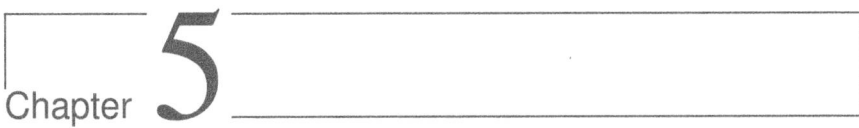

Chapter 5

Animated Articulated Characters

Everything is theoretically impossible, until it is done.

Robert A. Heinlein

5.1 Introduction

Animated characters are represented by collections of fixed length bones and joint angles. The character has a rigid skeleton frame (i.e., interconnected bones). Changing the joint angles over time enables us to simulate movement analogous to the real-world. We can limit the range of the joint angles to ensure the animation remains within the realm of realism - for example, we can't bend our knee backwards.

5.2 Articulated Skeleton

5.2.1 Bones (Root)

An articulated skeleton is composed of a collection of bones (i.e., rigid bodies). The bones are represented by simplified shapes, such as, rectangles and capsules.

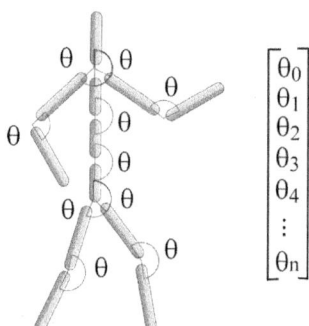

Figure 5.1. *Articulated Character - Character is composed of rigid limbs that are connected via joints - these joints have angles associated with them. As the joint angles change the character's pose changes. Changing the joint angles with time results in an animated character.*

Degrees of Freedom (DOF) A 2-dimensional unconstrained rigid body has 3 dof (2 translation and 1 rotation). A 3-dimensional unconstrained rigid body has 6 dof (3 translation and 6 rotation). If we have two unconstrained rigid bodies in a scene, we have sum the degrees of freedom, so we have 12 dof. However, if we add constraints, for example, this removes degrees of freedom, so adding a 'ball-joint' to connect two 3-dimensional rigid bodies, we would lose 3 dof - resulting in the scene having 9 dof. A character with 36 dof is sufficient to represent stylistic qualities.

How many bones are in the human body? The human body has 200+ bones. The tongue has 50+ bones in it alone. However, in character animations, typically a fraction of the number are used. As shown in Figure 5.1, twelve limbs is sufficient to represent most stylistic poses.

5.2.2 Hierarchy

The character limbs are connected in a hierarchy. The hierarchy has a root. A popular root for articulated character configurations is the pelvis. This means that small changes to joint angles lower in the hierarchy will affect inherited limbs. For instance, if the character moves the upper pelvis, the arms and hands will also move - hence, we must be aware of this if we are adapting the character pose to fit specific situations.

5.3 Skeletal Animation

A character pose is composed of an array of joint angles. The joint angles change with time. We can interpolate the angles to create smooth character animations.

5.3.1 Key-Frame Animations (Bone Data)

An array of key-frames are stored in a file. The key-frames represent a single static pose. Time frame information is assigned to each key-frames. We interpolate between the key-frames (i.e., joint angles) to create a smooth coherent motion.

5.3.2 Blending (Mixing Key-Frames)

While playing different animations at the same time and adding them together (i.e., joint angles), we are able to create an assortment of new animations. For example, mixing a walk and a run animation will produce an animation half way between running and walking. Another example, would be a walk animation and we mix in behavioural motions on top, such as, nervously looking around or stylistically swinging limbs (e.g., Ministry of Silly Walks).

5.4 Animation Data (Motion Capture)

Animated data for articulated characters is can come from a variety of sources. Either painstakingly created by an animation artist or from the recording of real-world human movement (i.e., motion capture). Motion capture data has the added advantage of being highly realistic and life-like.

5.4.1 File Formats

Lots of animation file formats exist. However, two popular motion capture file formats are the 'bvh' and 'asf/amc'. Both the asf/amc and bvh file formats are text based - so you can open them in your favourite text editor (e.g., notepad++) and view their contents.

5.4.2 ASF/AMC

The asf/amc motion capture file format stores the skeleton and key-frame data separately (e.g., see Listing 5.1 and Listing 5.2). Since we can have a single skeleton but a huge number of different animation types associated with it.

```
1   # AST/ASF file generated using VICON BodyLanguage
2   # ----------------------------------------------
3   :version 1.10
4   :name VICON
5   :units
6     mass 1.0
7     length 0.45
8     angle deg
9   :documentation
10    .ast/.asf automatically generated from VICON data using
11    VICON BodyBuilder and BodyLanguage model FoxedUp or BRILLIANT.MOD
12  :root
13    order TX TY TZ RX RY RZ
14    axis XYZ
15    position 0 0 0
16    orientation 0 0 0
17  :bonedata
18    begin
19      id 1
20      name lhipjoint
21      direction 0.692024 -0.648617 0.316857
22      length 2.68184
23      axis 0 0 0   XYZ
24    end
25    begin
26      id 2
27      name lfemur
28      direction 0.34202 -0.939693 0
29      length 6.92462
30      axis 0 0 20   XYZ
31      dof rx ry rz
32      limits (-160.0 20.0)
33             (-70.0 70.0)
34             (-60.0 70.0)
35    end
36    begin
37      id 3
38      name ltibia
39      direction 0.34202 -0.939693 0
40      length 7.40507
41      axis 0 0 20   XYZ
42      dof rx
43      limits (-10.0 170.0)
44    end
45    begin
46      id 4
47      name lfoot
48      direction 0.079671 -0.218894 0.972491
49      length 2.00008
50      axis -90 7.62852e-016 20   XYZ
51      dof rx rz
52      limits (-45.0 90.0)
53             (-70.0 20.0)
54    end
```

```
55
56     ....
57
58   :hierarchy
59     begin
60       root lhipjoint rhipjoint lowerback
61       lhipjoint lfemur
62       lfemur ltibia
63       ltibia lfoot
64       lfoot ltoes
65       rhipjoint rfemur
66       rfemur rtibia
67       rtibia rfoot
68       rfoot rtoes
69       lowerback upperback
70       upperback thorax
71       thorax lowerneck lclavicle rclavicle
72       lowerneck upperneck
73       upperneck head
74       lclavicle lhumerus
75       lhumerus lradius
76       lradius lwrist
77       lwrist lhand lthumb
78       lhand lfingers
79       rclavicle rhumerus
80       rhumerus rradius
81       rradius rwrist
82       rwrist rhand rthumb
83       rhand rfingers
84     end
```

Listing 5.1. Example of ASF file contents.

```
1    #commented out lines in an AMC file start with with a hash
2    :FULLY-SPECIFIED
3    :DEGREES
4    1
5      root 7.46593 15.9937 -36.7321 7.11356 1.31487 -3.66776
6      lowerback -4.29912 0.189404 0.939401
7      upperback -1.51886 0.185188 2.55702
8      thorax 0.845091 0.0960327 2.10705
9      lowerneck -18.6579 -5.17414 -13.3376
10     upperneck 13.6797 -6.63107 16.9236
11     head 8.38994 -2.28192 7.17028
12     rclavicle 6.33626e-015 1.59028e-014
13     rhumerus -38.7688 17.4551 -84.1031
14     rradius 56.1989
15     rwrist -28.5696
16     rhand -33.2015 -25.7513
17     rfingers 7.12502
18     rthumb -6.4087 -55.6344
19     lclavicle 6.33626e-015 1.59028e-014
20     lhumerus -35.9267 -2.97855 86.2544
21     lradius 27.4056
22     lwrist 7.30557
23     lhand -13.3003 -23.0211
24     lfingers 7.12502
25     lthumb 12.8038 6.56624
26     rfemur -9.89801 4.72659 30.1099
27     rtibia 24.1198
28     rfoot 0 0
```

39

```
29      rtoes 0
30      lfemur -40.6897 6.42258 -16.3516
31      ltibia 43.9106
32      lfoot -14.6186 8.34667
33      ltoes -11.8487
34  2
35      root 7.46979 15.9909 -36.6099 6.97364 1.17677 -3.42769
36      lowerback -4.02947 0.124717 0.686617
37      upperback -1.74341 0.122466 2.40941
38      thorax 0.46583 0.0663449 2.09235
39      lowerneck -18.3092 -4.94712 -12.866
40      upperneck 13.9808 -6.45508 16.5981
41      head 8.36631 -2.21315 7.00226
42      rclavicle 9.405e-015 1.19271e-015
43      rhumerus -39.2962 17.4621 -84.4896
44      rradius 56.9177
45      rwrist -29.7836
46      rhand -32.5089 -26.7042
47      rfingers 7.12502
48      rthumb -5.7401 -56.6064
49      lclavicle 9.405e-015 1.19271e-015
50      lhumerus -36.6135 -3.05608 86.2016
51      lradius 27.605
52      lwrist 7.3759
53      lhand -13.2527 -23.6778
54      lfingers 7.12502
55      lthumb 12.8496 5.90672
56      rfemur -9.10523 4.99331 29.8867
57      rtibia 23.7929
58      rfoot 0 0
59      rtoes 0
60      lfemur -40.6314 5.96489 -16.4186
61      ltibia 41.7651
62      lfoot -14.4396 7.79462
63      ltoes -11.6514
64  3
65      root 7.46865 15.9817 -36.4922 7.07496 1.02062 -3.42104
66      lowerback -4.25268 0.208491 0.534139
67      upperback -1.76783 0.23568 2.43554
68      thorax 0.561043 0.123555 2.21113
69      lowerneck -18.4858 -4.92439 -12.5804
70      upperneck 14.4563 -6.50752 16.431
71      head 8.54722 -2.22279 6.90035
72      rclavicle -1.70955e-014 7.95139e-016
73      rhumerus -39.3659 17.3532 -84.4603
74      rradius 57.625
75      rwrist -31.152
76      rhand -31.4625 -27.2739
77      rfingers 7.12502
78      rthumb -4.72972 -57.2011
79      lclavicle -1.70955e-014 7.95139e-016
80      lhumerus -36.5585 -3.05951 86.3507
81      lradius 27.3878
82      lwrist 7.04318
83      lhand -12.8526 -23.8908
84      lfingers 7.12502
85      lthumb 13.2353 5.66904
86      rfemur -8.43305 5.3581 29.9246
87      rtibia 23.264
88      rfoot 0 0
89      rtoes 0
90      lfemur -40.9779 5.65123 -16.2292
91      ltibia 39.9056
92      lfoot -14.4266 7.22118
93      ltoes -11.0794
```

Listing 5.2. Example of AMC file contents.

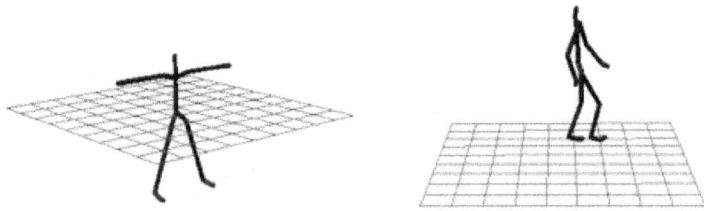

Figure 5.2. *ASF/AMC Loader/Renderer* - *Load seperate ASF skeleton and AMC mocap data - and combine them to render the animated skeleton.*

5.4.3 BVH

The bvh file format stores the skeleton information and key-frame animation data together in the same file (see Listing 5.3). At the beginning of the file is the hierarchy information, such as, limb lengths, names, and degrees of freedom, while at the end of the file are the key-frame animations.

```
 1  HIERARCHY
 2  ROOT Hips
 3  {
 4    OFFSET 0 0 0
 5    CHANNELS 6 Xposition Yposition Zposition Zrotation Yrotation ↩
        Xrotation
 6    JOINT LHipJoint
 7    {
 8      OFFSET 0 0 0
 9      CHANNELS 3 Zrotation Yrotation Xrotation
10      JOINT LeftHip
11      {
12        OFFSET 1.8559 -1.73949 0.84976
13        CHANNELS 3 Zrotation Yrotation Xrotation
14        JOINT LeftKnee
15        {
16          OFFSET 2.36836 -6.50702 0
17          CHANNELS 3 Zrotation Yrotation Xrotation
18          JOINT LeftAnkle
19          {
20            OFFSET 2.53268 -6.95849 0
21            CHANNELS 3 Zrotation Yrotation Xrotation
22            JOINT LeftToe
23            {
24              OFFSET 0.15935 -0.43781 1.94506
25              CHANNELS 3 Zrotation Yrotation Xrotation
```

```
26              End Site
27              {
28                OFFSET 0 0 1.00661
29              }
30            }
31          }
32        }
33      }
34    }
35    JOINT RHipJoint
36    {
37      OFFSET 0 0 0
38      CHANNELS 3 Zrotation Yrotation Xrotation
39      JOINT RightHip
40      {
41        OFFSET -1.68297 -1.73949 0.84976
42        CHANNELS 3 Zrotation Yrotation Xrotation
43        JOINT RightKnee
44        {
45          OFFSET -2.44709 -6.72334 0
46          CHANNELS 3 Zrotation Yrotation Xrotation
47          JOINT RightAnkle
48          {
49            OFFSET -2.43843 -6.69953 0
50            CHANNELS 3 Zrotation Yrotation Xrotation
51            JOINT RightToe
52            {
53              OFFSET -0.20854 -0.57295 2.02172
54              CHANNELS 3 Zrotation Yrotation Xrotation
55              End Site
56              {
57                OFFSET 0 0 1.05594
58              }
59            }
60          }
61        }
62      }
63    }
64    JOINT lowerback
65    {
66      OFFSET 0 0 0
67      CHANNELS 3 Zrotation Yrotation Xrotation
68      JOINT Chest
69      {
70        OFFSET -0.0156 2.23971 -0.03712
71        CHANNELS 3 Zrotation Yrotation Xrotation
72        JOINT Chest2
73        {
74          OFFSET 0.0549 2.19225 -0.19086
75          CHANNELS 3 Zrotation Yrotation Xrotation
76          JOINT lowerneck
77          {
78            OFFSET 0 0 0
79            CHANNELS 3 Zrotation Yrotation Xrotation
80            JOINT Neck
81            {
82              OFFSET -0.12403 1.43168 0.27585
83              CHANNELS 3 Zrotation Yrotation Xrotation
84              JOINT Head
85              {
86                OFFSET 0.17855 1.46173 -0.32578
87                CHANNELS 3 Zrotation Yrotation Xrotation
88                End Site
```

```
89             {
90                 OFFSET 0.07217 1.5159 -0.14537
91             }
92         }
93       }
94     }
95     . . .
96   }
97 }
98 }
99 MOTION
100 Frames: 316
101 Frame Time: 0.0083333
102 8.8721 15.7511 -31.7081 3.7012 4.912199 5.521699 0 0 0 -21.1091 ←
    17.2139 20.1408 0 0 0 -0.09899999 -6.7045 -1.5271 1.3585 ←
    -7.377699 -20.8392 0 0 0 13.256 12.8982 -36.9818 -2.505 ←
    -9.846999 28.4826 -0.0436 1.5354 -3.710599 -1.2054 6.9653 ←
    -19.6127 -6.683 -4.706999 -6.3678 2.0686 -5.8712 -0.6429999 ←
    5.2967 -3.0469 3.7868 -11.0665 -2.2708 -24.0759 11.8592 -2.4818←
    24.0856 6.0089 -0.5637 12.2401 0 0 0 8.773499 -27.8636 ←
    -42.9548 28.8308 -39.8699 10.6521 22.19 -27.5249 26.9772 0 0 0 ←
    -7.125 0 0 -4.7048 1.2657 -4.6154 0 0 0 -9.8517 15.5148 20.5834←
    -9.543599 -16.0225 -1.3462 -30.2032 7.6215 16.395 0 0 0 7.125 ←
    0 0 -2.3739 48.7658 0.2206
103 8.8482 15.7496 -31.4727 2.967 4.900499 5.448299 0 0 0 -19.8956 ←
    17.3922 20.9007 0 0 0 -0.0662 -4.6771 0.5881 1.1289 -6.7484 ←
    -18.972 0 0 0 14.2768 13.0139 -36.6217 -2.6367 -10.0823 29.2438←
    -0.0174 1.0964 -2.3527 -1.0129 6.4032 -17.959 -6.286799 ←
    -4.8082 -5.849699 2.594 -6.090799 -1.1548 5.6652 -3.1195 3.011 ←
    -11.4659 -2.0109 -24.2118 12.1627 -2.0853 24.8749 6.319 -0.3926←
    12.527 0 0 8.0221 -25.7306 -42.2848 29.5535 -40.5076 11.1185←
    22.2369 -
104 . . . .
```

Listing 5.3. Example BVH file contents.

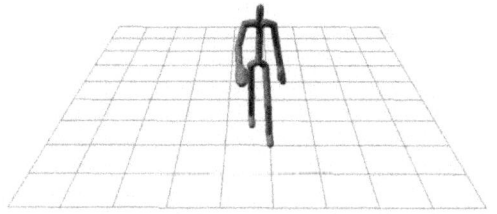

Figure 5.3. *BVH Motion Capture* - *Playing back the bvh file format data using capsules to represent the limbs (bones).*

5.5 Skinning

When a mesh is wrapped over the rigid body skeleton to create a more aesthetically pleasing effect. Similar to how we as humans have skin and tissue wrapped over our bones. Each skin vertex is attached to bones using a scalar weighting. As the bone moves it influences the vertex skin. So multiple bones can connect a single vertex (as with the knee and elbow). This means our character is covered with a single 'skin mesh' that deforms and follows the underlying skeleton bones.

5.5.1 Weighting (attaching the skin to bones)

A single mesh encapsulates the character limbs. Different limbs are attached to the skin with 'weighted' values that determine the bones influence on the skin. The sum of the weights should add up to 1.0. So if two bones equally effect a vertex - each bone would contribute 0.5 (50%) towards the skin vertex's final position.

Dual-Quaternions When limbs are bent sharply they will create visual artifacts (i.e., 'kinks') in the graphical skinning mesh. One solution to reduce this, is to used weighted dual-quaternions. While quaternions are used to represent rotation, dual-quaternions are an extension to this concept using dual-number theory and allow both translation and rotation to be represented. Dual-quaternions have the added benefit of when they are used in skinning and blended together, they solve the 'kinking' problem - instead producing a more rounder nicer looking solution.

5.5.2 File Formats (.x, .b3d, .collada, .fbx)

While animation formats, such as, bvh and asf/amc contain only skeletal animation information, other formats, such as, .x and .fbx, are able to contain an assortment of character data - for instance, skinning, texturing, and animation information.

5.6 Summary

Animated characters are an essential resource in virtual environments. We have covered the 'kinematic' properties of motion for articulated bodies. In later chapters, we expand these concepts to include procedural and dynamic methods (e.g., collisions, physics, and ragdolls).

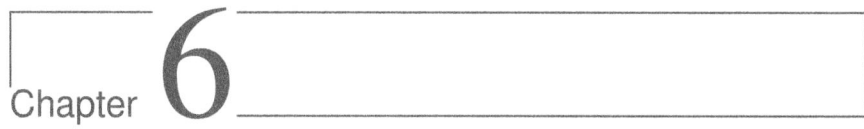

Chapter 6

Particle Physics

The science of today is the technology of tomorrow.

Edward Teller

6.1 Introduction

Particle physics allows a scene to be more interactive and engaging. Particles introduces life into a scene. Particles visually show forces, such as, wind and dust movement. It would be impossible to store the movement of each particle over time, instead, we store force fields and control forces. Particles are able to represent a large repertoire of dynamic effects, to name just a few: fire, water, rain, dust, leaves, sparks, clouds, and smoke.

Parameters We specify a number of parameters for each particle. The parameters depend upon the type of effect we are trying to create. A few possible parameters are:

- life-span - after a specified amount of time the particle will fade away
- alpha - transparency will change over time
- color - fixed or changing color
- texture - either animated or fixed texture

- emit-rate - how often new particles are emitted and their starting location and values
- velocity - initial velocity

6.2 Particles (Point-Masses)

A particle is a simple graphical object used as a visual enhancement. Particles enable the creation of a huge number of graphical effects, such as, fire, smoke, dust, and sparks.

Integration A network of point-masses are controlled using forces, such as, external user input or constraints, like springs and collisions. Through Newton's 2nd law we are able to calculate the acceleration of every point-mass at any given time (i.e., $f = m\,a$) - where f is the force, m is the mass, and a the acceleration. The mass remains constant and the acceleration is calculated from the forces (i.e., $a = f/m$), while the 'integration' step is used to compute the 'actual motion'.

$$\frac{d\vec{x}}{dt} = \vec{v}$$
$$\frac{d^2\vec{x}}{dt^2} = \frac{d\vec{x}}{dt} \tag{6.1}$$
$$= \frac{1}{m}(\vec{F}_{gravity} + \vec{F}_{damping} + \vec{F}_{external})$$

where x is the point-mass position, v is the point-mass velocity, and f is the sum of the applied forces. Equation 6.1 describe the movement of a single point-mass. We apply the equation to all the point-masses and obtain a system of ordinary differential equations (ODEs). In general, it is impossible to solve the problem analytically and must be solved numerically. Methods to solve such systems numerically are called 'integrators'. The most widely used integrators are: Euler 1st order, Runge-Kutta 2nd order (aka the midpoint method) and Runge-Kutta 4th order (RK4).

To achieve a real-time frame-rates, we focus on a simple first order particle integrator. We begin by introducing a particle simulator using Newtonian mechanics (i.e., $f = ma$). Hence, each particle needs to have:

- position
- acceleration
- mass

However, since we are constantly calculating 1/mass, it's more convenient and computationally faster to store the inverse mass (i.e., *invmass*).

Differentiation is used to represent the 'rate-of-change' of something (i.e., change in position with time - velocity) - while integration is used to find the opposite (i.e., how the velocity causes a change in position). We apply forces to our particles, either from wind or from neighbouring constraints. From Newton's second law (i.e., $f = ma$), we can derive the acceleration. Integrating the acceleration with respect to time gives us the velocity. Integrating the velocity with respect to time gives us the position. This provides a relationship that we use to predict how the velocity and position change with respect to time in relation to the applied forces.

Euler Integration A popular first order approximation method is the Euler integration scheme, shown below in Equation 6.2:

$$v_{n+1} = v_n + a\, dt$$
$$p_{n+1} = p_n + v_{n+1}\, dt \tag{6.2}$$

However, for the simulation to remain stable and realistic, the time-step must be extremely small and the forces (i.e., accelerations) must remain within reasonable limits. Since we're interested in real-time interactive environments (e.g., games), stability is important. Later, we will explain how to modify the first order Euler equation to formulate a verlet integrator (i.e., a velocity-less system) to create a more stable and efficient technique. We show a simple implementation of a particle in Listing 6.1.

```
1   class Particle // 'Newtonian' Particle Integration
2   {
3       Vector3 m_pos;
4       Vector3 m_vel;
5       Vector3 m_force;
6       float   m_invMass;
7   public:
8           Particle (const Vector3& p)
9       void Update    (float dt);
10      void AddForce (const Vector3& f);
11
12  };//End class Particle
13
14
15  Particle::Particle(const Vector3& p) : m_pos(p)
16  {
17      m_vel    = Vector3(0,0,0);
18      m_force  = Vector3(0,0,0);
19      m_invMass = 1.0f;
20  }// End Particle()
21
22  void Particle::Update(float dt)
23  {
24      m_vel += m_force * m_invMass * dt;
25      m_pos += m_vel * dt;
26      m_force = Vector3(0,0,0);
27  }// End Update(..)
```

```
28
29  void Particle::AddForce(const Vector3& f)
30  {
31    m_force += f;
32  }// End AddForce(..)
```

Listing 6.1. Simple particle class using simple Newtonian mechanics.

6.2.1 Magnetic 'Control' Forces

We control the motion of particles through forces. 'Magnetic' forces steer the trajectory of particles. For example, if we want create a 'tornado' of particles that twist and twirl in a circular vortex-like pattern.

6.2.2 Billboarding

A visual illusion is to have each particle map onto a quad. The quad is draw so that it always faces the camera. This creates the illusion of a solid object. Reducing the memory and computational overhead of rendering a complex geometric object - since a quad requires only four vertices and two triangles, as shown in Figure 6.1.

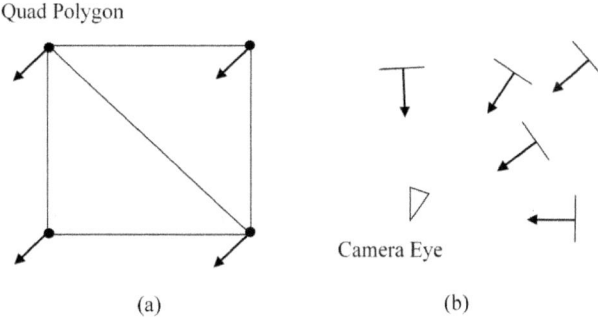

(a) (b)

Figure 6.1. *Billboarding - Visual illusion of always having the quad face towards the camera eye.*

The texture on the quad depend upon the effect, for example:
- Leaves
- Clouds
- Dust
- Sparks
- ...

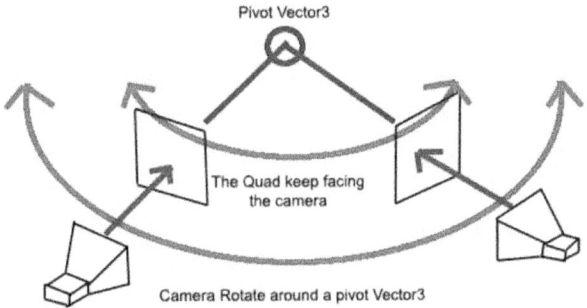

Figure 6.2. ***Billboarding*** *- An visual trick to create the illusion of depth by having a quad always face towards the camera.*

6.3 Coupled Particles

We can connect particles together using simple distance constraints to create a complex dynamic system, such as, soft bodies, clothes and plant vegetation.

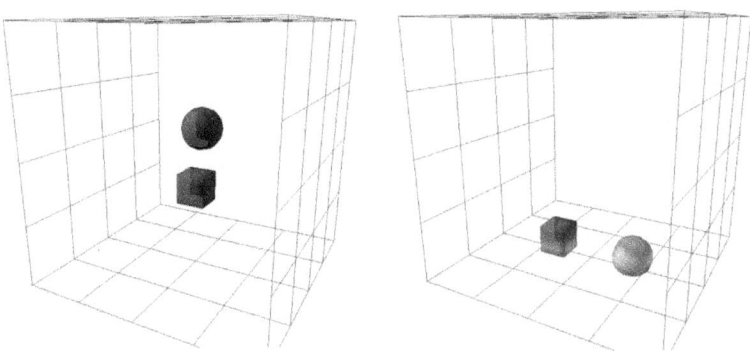

Figure 6.3. ***Soft Bodies*** *- Coupled particles connected via springs enable us to create soft body shapes. Screen capture of a sphere and cube bouncing around within a bounding axis aligned box.*

Hooke's Springs The first method for connecting particles is with 'penalty' forces. Particles are connected together via a fixed length. At each frame we can calculate the current distance between the constrained particles. If the length is greater than the originally specified fixed length, we apply a correcting penalty force to pull the particles back together. While if the

49

particles move to close together, we apply a penalty force to push them apart. An example implementation is given below in Listing 6.2:

```
1
2  class HookeSpringConstraint
3  {
4  private:
5  // the length between particles p1 and p2 in rest
6  // configuration
7  float rest_distance;
8  // the two particles that are connected through
9  // this constraint
10 Particle *p1, *p2;
11
12
13 public:
14
15 HookeSpringConstraint(Particle *p1, Particle *p2) :  p1(p1),p2(p2)
16 {
17   // Make sure both particles aren't the same
18   DBG_ASSERT( p1 != p2 );
19   // Make sure that both particle pointers are
20   // valid (i.e., not NULL)
21   DBG_ASSERT( p1 != NULL );
22   DBG_ASSERT( p2 != NULL );
23
24   Vector3 vec = p1->GetPos() - p2->GetPos();
25   rest_distance = vec.Length();
26 }// End HookeSpringConstraint(..)
27
28 // This is one of the important methods, where a
29 // single constraint between two particles p1 and p2
30 // is solved the method is called each frame
31 void UpdateConstraint(float dt)
32 {
33   // Typical form:
34   //
35   // F = - ks x - kd v
36   //
37   // where kd is the coefficient of damping and v is the
38   // relative velocity between the two points connected
39   // by the spring. Larger values for kd increase the
40   // amount of damping so the object will come to rest
41   // more quickly.
42   //
43   // For 3D space we represent the typical form as:
44   //
45   // F = -ks (|x|-d)(x/|x|) - kd v
46   //
47   // Where |x| is the distance between the two points
48   // connected to the spring, d is the desired distance
49   // of separation, and x / |x| is the unit length
50   // direction vector between the two points: a to b,
51   // when applying the force to point a and vice versa.
52
53   // More complicated damping is also possible,
54   // including damping proportional to an objects
55   // squared velocity, as well logarithmic functions.
56   // We focus here on simple linear damping.
57
58   // default spring-damping constants
```

```
59    const float khook = 5.0f;
60    const float kdamp = khook*0.0001f;
61
62    // vector from p1 to p2
63    Vector3 p1_to_p2      = p2->GetPos()-p1->GetPos();
64    // current distance between p1 and p2
65    float      current_distance      = p1_to_p2.Length();
66
67    // # 1 - Compute hook force
68    float    stretchDist = current_distance - rest_distance;
69    Vector3 normal = Vector3::Normalize(p1_to_p2);
70    Vector3 fhook  = normal * stretchDist * khook;
71
72    // # 2 - Compute damping force
73    // i.e., damping is opposite to the relative velocity
74    // To incorporate damping into the spring equation,
75    // we first find the relative velocity between the
76    // two connected particles 1 and 2. We define
77    // relative velocity as:
78    Vector3 relvel = p2->GetVelocity() - p1->GetVelocity();
79
80    // We now have the relative velocity of particle 2
81    // with respect to object 1. Further, we only want to
82    // dampen motion along the axis of the spring. That
83    // is, we only care about the component of vrel
84    // which lies in the direction of normal. To find this
85    // quantity, we must project the vector vrel onto
86    // normal ; because we have defined normal as a unit
87    // vector, the projection amounts to a dot product.
88    // Our final damping term acting on object 2 then is:
89
90    float    dampAmount = Vector3::Dot( normal, relvel );
91    Vector3 fdamp    = normal * dampAmount * kdamp;
92
93    // # 3 - Add forces together and apply them to the
94    // particles:
95    p1->AddForce(  fhook + fdamp );
96    p2->AddForce(  -fhook - fdamp );
97
98  }// End UpdateConstraint(..)
99
100
101   // Draw the constraint - i.e. a simple line between
102   // the two particles
103   void Draw()
104   {
105     DrawLine( p1->GetPos(), p2->GetPos() );
106   }// End Draw(..)
107
108 }; // End HookeSpringConstraint
```

Listing 6.2. Hooke spring constraint implementation example - for a basic Newtonian particle system.

Engineering Design Tips

- Numerical stability issues

For large time-steps the system will 'explode' (e.g., dt = 0.001 is a good starting choice)

Euler is much more unstable compared to RK2 or RK4, but requires smaller time-steps while being simpler and faster

Euler is rarely used in practice (i.e., typically RK4)

Smaller time-steps means more stability and accuracy (but also means more computation)

- For springs constraints - the time-step should be inversely proportional to the square root of the elasticity k [Courant condition]
- Computational cost (i.e., trade-off: accuracy vs computation-time)
- Be aware of floating point and double precision calculation errors
- Choosing the right elasticity and damping parameters is an art (i.e., trial and error). Initially, set the ordinary and collision parameters the same to create a stable simulation

Springs/Verlet (Distance Constraints)   Velocity approximation approach using a 'verlet' integration scheme allows us to create a robust constraint based solution. We use the current and previous position for each particle. Upon integrating each particle forward each frame (i.e., accumulated forces). The constraints are enforced by 'snapping' the positions back into place. The verlet integration scheme is derived in Equation 6.4 below:

$$v_{n+1} = v_n + a\ dt$$
$$p_{n+1} = p_n + v_{n+1}\ dt \tag{6.3}$$

Combine Equation 6.3 into a single equation:

$$p_{n+1} = p_n + (v_n + a\ dt)\ dt$$
$$= p_n + v_n dt + a\ dt^2 \tag{6.4}$$

where v represents the velocity, p the position, a acceleration, and dt the timestep, while the subscript n and $n+1$ dictates the current and next frame. With the verlet scheme, we approximate velocity using the current and previous position (see Equation6.5):

$$v_n = \frac{p_n - p_{n-1}}{dt} \tag{6.5}$$

Substituting Equation 6.5 into Equation 6.4:

$$p_{n+1} = p_n + \left(\frac{p_n - p_{n-1}}{dt}\right) dt + a \, dt^2$$
$$= p_n + (p_n - p_{n-1}) + a \, dt^2 \tag{6.6}$$
$$= 2 \, p_n - p_{n-1} + a \, dt^2$$

Equation 6.6, is our verlet integration scheme - notice the next frame (p_{n+1}) is only dependant on the current and previous position (i.e., it does not store or use any velocity parameters). Hence, it is sometimes referred to as a velocity-less or position-based integration technique.

Verlet Damping   We don't want our system to oscillate forever - instead we want our particles to lose energy (e.g., through air resistance and friction). We modify our verlet Equation 6.6 to include damping, as shown below in Equation 6.7:

$$p_{n+1} = p_n + (p_n - p_{n-1})(1 - c) + (a \, dt^2) \tag{6.7}$$

where c is a scalar damping coefficient between 0.0 and 1.0 - with 1.0 causing 100% damping and no movement, while a damping coefficient of zero adds no damping - typically we use a value of around 0.01 in practice.

```
1   class Particle // ``Verlet'' Particle Integration
2   {
3   private:
4   // can the particle move or not -
5   // to pin parts particles in the scene
6   bool movable;
7   // the invmass of the particle
8   float invmass;
9   // the current position of the particle in 3D space
10  Vector3 pos;
11  // the position of the particle in the previous time
12  // step, used as part of the verlet numerical
13  // integration scheme
14  Vector3 oldPos;
15  // vector for the current acceleration of the particle
16  Vector3 acceleration;
17
18  public:
19  Particle(const Vector3& pos) :
20      pos(pos),
21      oldPos(pos),
22      acceleration(Vector3(0,0,0)),
23      invmass(1),
24      movable(true) {}
25
26  // This is one of the important methods,
27  // where the time is progressed a single step size (dt2)
28  // Given the equation f=ma, i.e.,
29  // ``force = mass * acceleration'' the
```

```
30  // next position is found through
31  // verlet integration
32  void Integrate(float dt)
33  { // e.g., DAMPING = 0.01f
34    if (!movable) return;
35
36    Vector3 temp = pos;
37    pos = pos + (pos-oldPos)*(1.0f-DAMPING) + acceleration*dt*dt;
38    oldPos = temp;
39    // acceleration is reset since it HAS been translated
40    // into a change in position (and implicitely
41    // into velocity)
42    acceleration = Vector3(0,0,0);
43
44  }// End Integrate(..)
45
46  void AddForce(const Vector3& f)
47  {
48  // i.e., Newton's second law: f = m a
49  acceleration += f * invmass;
50  }// End AddForce(..)
51
52  Vector3 GetPos() const { return pos; }
53
54  void MakeUnmovable () { movable = false; }
55
56  }; // End Particle(..)
```

As shown in Algorithm 1, we need to update the verlet constraints inside a loop. This is because, as we correct one constraint by snapping it back into position, it will cause another constraint to be violated. However, the system will converge on an acceptable solution after a number of iterations. Fewer iterations results in the constraints appearing soft - this is rectified by more adding more iterations to increase rigidity.

Algorithm 1 Verlet constraint algorithm - important to note we 'snap' the particles to ensure constraints are enforced (i.e., we move their position). For example, when a particle penetrates the ground, we simply move the particle out of collision with the ground and integrate forward.

1: Add forces to each particle
2: Integrate each particle forward by dt
3: **while** Error exists or maximum number of iterations **do**
4:     Calculate distance constraint error and 'move' particle out of error
5: **end while**

```
1
2  class VerletDistanceConstraint
3  {
4  private:
5  // the length between particles p1 and p2 in rest
6  // configuration
7  float restDistance;
8  // the two particles that are connected through
```

```
 9  // this constraint
10  Particle *p1, *p2;
11
12  public:
13
14  VerletDistanceConstraint(Particle *p1, Particle *p2) :
15      p1(p1),p2(p2)
16  {
17      // Make sure both particles aren't the same
18      DBG_ASSERT( p1 != p2 );
19      // Make sure that both particle pointers are
20      // valid (i.e., not NULL)
21      DBG_ASSERT( p1 != NULL );
22      DBG_ASSERT( p2 != NULL );
23
24      Vector3 vec = p1->GetPos() - p2->GetPos();
25      restDistance = vec.Length();
26
27  }// End VerletDistanceConstraint(..)
28
29  // This is one of the important methods, where a
30  // single constraint between two particles p1 and p2
31  // is solved the method is called each frame
32  void UpdateConstraint(float dt)
33  {
34
35      // vector from p1 to p2
36      Vector3 p1_to_p2      = p2->GetPos()-p1->GetPos();
37      // current distance between p1 and p2
38      float currentDistance     = p1_to_p2.Length();
39
40      // # 1 - Compute correcting distance
41      float   moveDist = current_distance - rest_distance;
42      Vector3 normal   = Vector3::Normalize(p1_to_p2);
43
44      // # 2 - Apply correction to the particles:
45      p1->oldPos += normal * moveDist * 0.5f;
46      p2->oldPos -= normal * moveDist * 0.5f;
47
48  }// End UpdateConstraint(..)
49
50
51  // Draw the constraint - i.e. a simple line between
52  // the two particles
53  void Draw()
54  {
55      DrawLine( p1->GetPos(), p2->GetPos() );
56  }// End Draw(..)
57
58  }; // End VerletDistanceConstraint
```

Listing 6.3. Verlet distance constraint implementation example - for a basic verlet particle system.

6.3.1 Cloth/Soft Body Animation Systems

A fun simulation technique is that of cloth and soft-bodies. Essentially, every neighbouring particle is connected together with a distance constraint. The more constraints make the system more rigid.

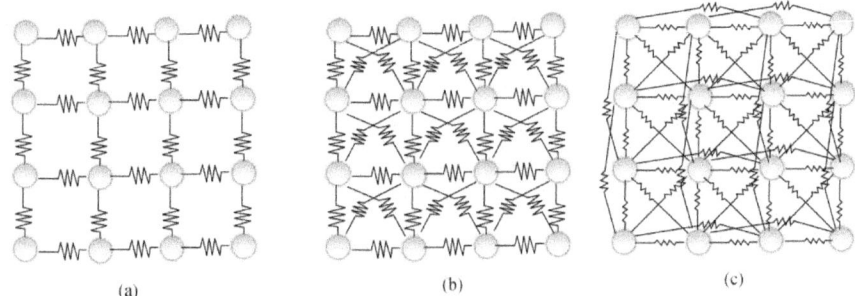

(a)   (b)   (c)

Figure 6.4. *Cloth Topology* - *We can keep adding additional constraints to create the effect we are looking for in our cloth - for example, adding sheer and bend springs so the cloth is more 'smooth' and less sharp when bending (i.e., influence over a larger area instead of just the neighbours).*

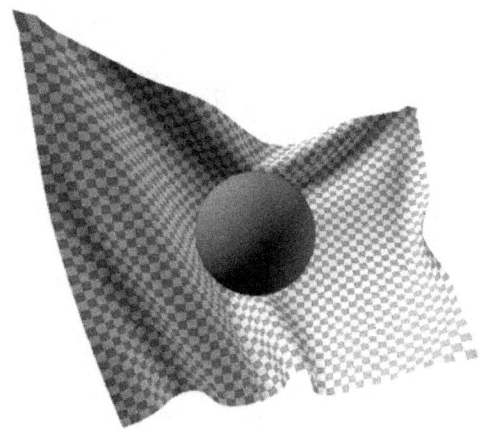

Figure 6.5. *Cloth Simulation* - *Simple verlet cloth simulation screen capture - 140 particles - with wind forces and sheer, structural, and bend.*

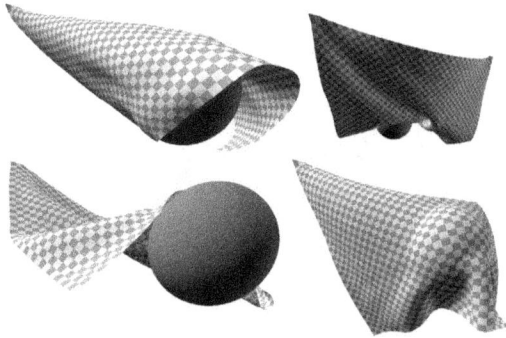

Figure 6.6. *Cloth Simulation* - *Real-time interactive cloth simulation screen capture.*

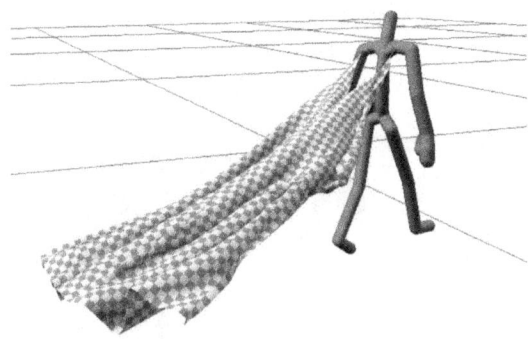

Figure 6.7. *Cloth Simulation* - *Attaching the cloth to an animated character.*

57

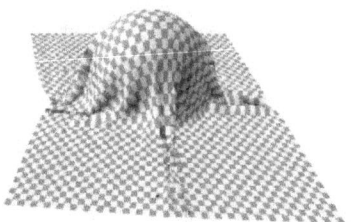

Figure 6.8. *Cloth Simulation* - *Wrapping cloth around rigid body objects.*

6.3.2 Vegetation (Trees/Plants)

We can connect particles together using constraints to represent plant and tree topologies. Mapping textures for leaves and other foliage. Adding in external forces, such as, wind enables us to create trees and plants that sway and oscillate in an organic life-like manner.

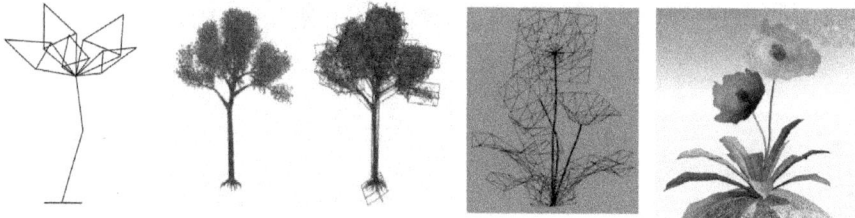

Figure 6.9. *Vegetation* - *Dynamic plants.*

Interestingly, we could use a procedural algorithm to generate the plant/vegetation (e.g., trees, grass, or leaves) - enabling us to quickly and effectively add both detailed plants to a scene that move in response to disturbances.

6.4 Ragdolls from Particle

We can connect particles together in a triangle configurations so we can extract orientation information (i.e., 3-dimensional rotation). The orientation information in combination with the positions can be used to represent limbs on an articulated character.

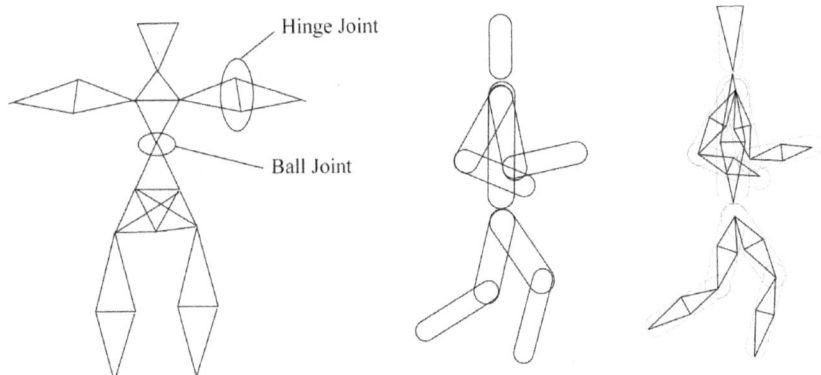

Figure 6.10. ***Ragdoll from Particles*** - *Connecting particles together in a specific configurations enables us to create a rigid character skeleton. We can use the fact that a 'triangle' will always keep its shape. The triangle structure enables us to extract position and orientation information for the graphical character mesh.*

6.5 Particle Orientation

Technically, a point mass with an orientation is a 'rigid body'. A rigid body has both linear and angular properties. However, we can create a kinematic orientation for aesthetic qualities. For example, a trigonometric orientation based on the translational value - or a simple linearly changing orientation - for the graphical output.

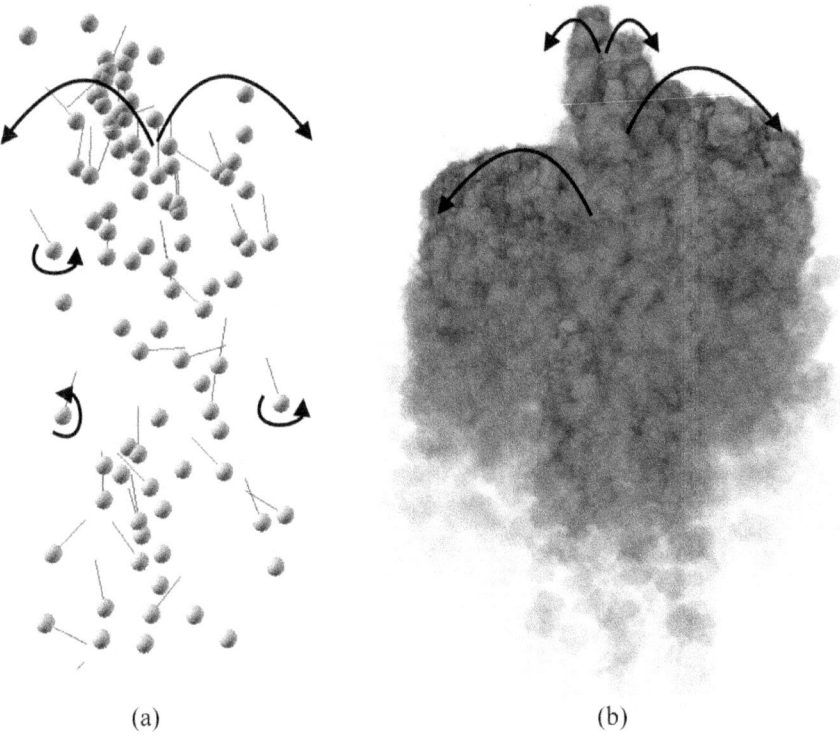

(a)   (b)

Figure 6.11. *Particle Billboarding/Rotation - Simple program shows a bare-bone particle system; (a) simple point-mass particles with an ad-hoc spinning motion, and (b) a billboarded textured smoke effect.*

6.6 Summary

This chapter has only scratched the potential of simple physics based solutions for adding enhanced visual realism to a scene. In the next chapter, we continue with physics based principles and expanding the concept of particles to include basic rigid body mechanics.

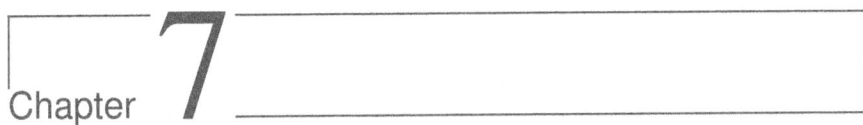

Chapter 7

Rigid Bodies and Ragdolls

The distance between insanity and genius is measured only by success.

Bruce Feirstein

7.1 Introduction

We introduce the basic rigid body mechanics necessary to simulate a simple rigid body system. The rigid body system is used to simulate a character rag-doll implementation. A rigid body builds upon the simple physical mechanics of a particle from the previous chapter, but we add rotational components (i.e., both linear and angular forces and velocities). Rigid bodies enable us to simulate the movement of solid objects - including collisions, friction, and constraints - ranging from ragdolls, collapsing buildings, bridges, and more. The key topics we cover in this chapter are:

- Collision Detection (including contact information)
- Classical Mechanics (Newton's laws, rigid bodies, mass, integration)
- Constraints (distance constraints, springs, Hooke's law)
- Collisions (penalty-springs)
- Rigid Body Ragdolls
- Inverse Kinematics
- Inverse Dynamics

7.2 Collision Detection

7.2.1 Contact Information

After determining if we have a collision, we also need to calculate contact information. The contact information tells us how to resolve the collision, for example, if the two objects are overlapping, then what is the most best way to push them out of separation. The three main piece of contact information we calculate are:

- Contact normal - direction to move the two objects out of penetration (normalized vector)
- Contact point - position of the two points (vector)
- Penetration depth - overlapping penetration depth (scalar)

7.2.2 Capsules

Capsules are an efficient method for representing an approximate boundary. We represent capsules by a line and a radius.

Capsule-Capsule

We calculate the capsule-capsule collision detection information by first determining the shortest distance between two lines. If the distance between the two lines is less than the sum of the radii of the two capsules, we have a collision, and we continue to calculate the contact information.

Parametric Equation for Line   We go through the steps of solving the problem of determining the intersection point of two parametric lines.

$$P(s) = A + (B - A)s$$
$$R(t) = X + (Y - X)t$$

let:

$$B - A = N \tag{7.1}$$
$$Y - X = M$$
$$P(s) = A + Ns$$
$$R(t) = X + Mt$$

Intersect same point they should be equal, hence $P(s) = R(t)$:

$$A + Ns = X + Mt \tag{7.2}$$

We have two unknowns and one equation, which we solve by doing the cross product both sides by M to remove an unknown:

$$(A \times M) + (Ns \times M) = (X \times M) + (Mt \times M)$$
$$(A \times M) + (Ns \times M) = (X \times M)$$

(7.3)

Only one unknown now, so solve for s:

$$Ns \times M = (X \times M) - (A \times M)$$
$$s(N \times M) = (X \times M) - (A \times M)$$
$$s(N \times M) \cdot (N \times M) = ((X \times M) - (A \times M)) \cdot (N \times M)$$

(7.4)

$$s = \frac{((X \times M) - (A \times M)) \cdot (N \times M)}{(N \times M) \cdot (N \times M)}$$

We do the same for t so we have the two unknowns for the intersection point of two parametric lines. We 'clamp' s and t to 0 and the length of the lines. We substitute the values back into our parametric line given in Equation 7.1 to work out the two closest points.

$$s = \frac{((X \times (Y - X)) - (A \times (Y - X))) \cdot ((A - B) \times (Y - X))}{((A - B) \times (Y - X)) \cdot ((A - B) \times (Y - X))}$$

$$t = \frac{((A \times (B - A)) - (X \times (B - A))) \cdot ((Y - X) \times (A - B))}{((Y - X) \times (A - B)) \cdot ((Y - X) \times (A - B))}$$

(7.5)

$$P(s) = A + (B - A)s$$
$$R(t) = X + (Y - X)t$$

(7.6)

The calculation for s and t appears complex from Equation 7.5, however, the operations are just simple cross and dot products. Furthermore, we can simplify the cost by performing similar calculations once. For example, the divider in both equations are the same but reversed, which we can calculate once and add a negative sign - see Listing 7.1, for an example implementation.

```
1  bool CapsuleCapsuleIntersection(const Vector3& A, const Vector3& B, ↩
       float radiusA,
2                 const Vector3& X, const Vector3& Y, float radiusX,
3                 Vector3* outCP, // out contact point
4                 Vector3* outCN, // out contact normal
5                 float*   outPD) // out penetration depth
6  {
7    const Vector3 N = B - A;
8    const Vector3 M = Y - X;
9
```

```
10    Vector3 bottom = Vector3::Cross(N, M);
11
12    float bs = Vector3::Dot(bottom, bottom);
13
14    float s = Vector3::Dot( Vector3::Cross(X,M) - Vector3::Cross(A,Y-X↩
          ),    bottom ) / bs;
15
16    float t = Vector3::Dot( Vector3::Cross(A,N) - Vector3::Cross(X,B-A↩
          ),   -bottom ) / bs;
17
18    s = Clamp(s, 0.0f, 1.0f);
19    t = Clamp(t, 0.0f, 1.0f);
20
21    Vector3 P = A + N * s;
22    Vector3 R = X + M * t;
23
24    float dist = Vector3::Length( P - R );
25
26    if ( dist > radiusA + radiusX )
27    {
28    // No collision
29    return false;
30    }
31
32    // If here - we have a collision so we need to
33    // calculate the contact information
34
35    // Contact normal
36    (*outCN) = Vector3::Normalize(P-R);
37
38    // Contact point
39    (*outCP) = (P+R)*0.5f;
40
41    // Penetration depth
42    (*outPD) = dist - (radiusA + radiusX);
43
44    return true;// Collision
45 }// End CapsuleCapsuleIntersection(..)
```

Listing 7.1. Example capsule-capsule intersection implementation (note for simplicity we have excluded sanity checks and error checking (e.g., parallel lines)).

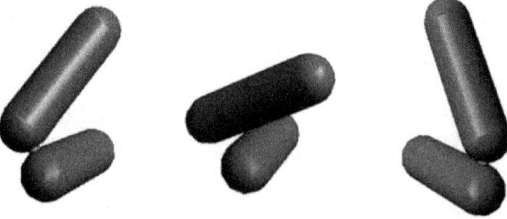

Figure 7.1. *Capsule-Capsule* - *Testing capsule-capsule collision detection/contact calculations by drawing the contact point as a red sphere.*

Capsule-Plane

We combine the parametric equation of a line with the plane equation to determine the shortest distance between a point and a line. If the distance is less than the radius of the capsule, we have an intersection and proceed to calculate the contact information (i.e., the contact normal, contact point, and penetration depth).

Plane Equation Plane equation defines the shortest distance for the plane to the origin, as given below in Equation 7.7:

$$d = n \cdot p \tag{7.7}$$

where n is the plane normal, p is any point on the plane, and d is shortest distance to origin from the plane.

Line-Plane Point on a line using the parametric line equation:

$$P(t) = A + (B - A)t \tag{7.8}$$

where $P(t)$ is the point on the line, A is the start of the line, B is the end of the line, and t is a scalar from 0.0 to 1.0.

We substitute the point on a line from the parametric representation given in Equation 7.8 into the plane equation given in Equation 7.7.

$$d = n \cdot p$$
$$d = 0 \quad \text{when on the plane}$$

subtitute for p:
$$n \cdot (A + (B - A)t) = 0$$

solve for t:
$$\tag{7.9}$$
$$(n \cdot A) + (n \cdot (B - A)t) = 0$$
$$t = \frac{-n \cdot A}{n \cdot (B - A)}$$

We clamp the value for the line-plane equation to length of the line. We can substitute the value back into the line equation to fine the closest point to the plane. If the distance between the point and the plane is less than the radius of the capsule, we have a collision.

```
1  bool CapsulePlaneIntersection(const Vector3& A, const Vector3& B, ↩
       float radiusA,
2                   const Vector3& P, const Vector3& n,
3                   Vector3* outCP, // out contact point
4                   Vector3* outCN, // out contact normal
5                   float*   outPD) // out penetration depth
6  {
7    float t = Vector3::Dot( -n, A ) / Vector3::Dot( n, B-A );
8
9    t = Clamp( t, 0.0f, 1.0f );
10
11   Vector3 closestPoint = A + (B-A)*t;
12
13   // Calculate the distance between the closest point
14   // and the plane
15   float d = Vector3::Dot(n, closestPoint) - Vector3::Dot(n, p);
16
17   if ( d > radiusA )
18   {
19   // No collision
20   return false;
21   }
22
23   // We have a collision so calculate the contact
24   // information (i.e., point on the plane)
25
26   *outCN = n;
27   *outPD = radiusA - d;
28   *outCP = closestPoint - n*d;
29
30   return true; // Collision
31  }// End CapsulePlaneIntersection(..)
```

Listing 7.2. Example capsule-plane intersection implementation (note for simplicity we have excluded sanity checks and error checking (e.g., parallel line-plane)).

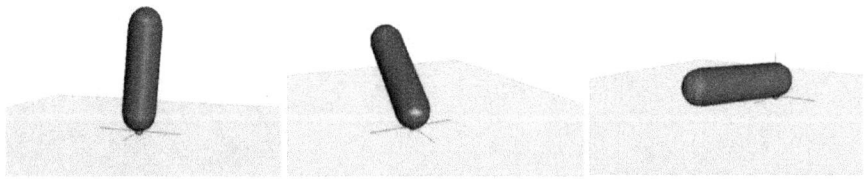

Figure 7.2. *Capsule-Plane - Testing capsule-plane collision detection/-contact calculations by drawing the contact data as a red sphere/cross.*

Practical Collision/Contact Considerations We only calculate a single contact point - hence, the shape will 'jitter' around on the ground as the contact point jumps between ends. This can be resolved by 'caching' the contact points each frame to build up a contact manifold .

7.3 Basic Rigid Body Mechanics

Forces & Torques (Newton & Euler) The equations of motion for an un-constrained rigid body are governed by the fundamental laws of mechanics (classical mechanics) .

Linear

$$f = ma$$

Angular

$$\tau = I\alpha$$

(7.10)

where f is force, m is mass, a linear acceleration, τ is torque, I angular inertia, and α is angular acceleration. Note, we use the light weight version of τ - as technically in 3-dimensions, we would have angular effects, such as Coriolis, which we have excluded.

Friction Motion is created through forces and torques - this also includes resistance to motion. Hence, if we want to stop an object sliding or slipping along a surface, in addition to calculating the collision forces, we also need to calculate the tangential frictional forces. The frictional force is a force that acts against the objects velocity at the point of contact (i.e., the surface contact point velocities).

Connecting Linear & Angular Forces We connect the linear and angular forces via Equation 7.11 below:

$$\tau = r \times f$$

(7.11)

where τ is the torque induced by the applying force f and r is the offset vector from the centre of mass that the force is being applied. Note the equation is for 3-dimensions and $\times$ is the cross product.

Mass & Inertia Mass represents the resistance to change in motion. In 2-dimensions the mass and inertia are represented by a scalar. In 3-dimensions the mass is represented by a scalar, however, the inertia is represented by a 3×3 matrix.

Integration

$$\text{change in velocity} = \int acceleration$$

$$\text{change in position} = \int velocity \tag{7.12}$$

```
1   class RigidBody
2   {
3   public:
4       // Linear
5       Vector3    m_position;
6       Vector3    m_linVelocity;
7       float      m_invMass;
8       Vector3    m_force;
9
10      // Angular
11      Quaternion m_orientation;
12      Vector3    m_angVelocity;
13      Matrix4    m_invLocalInertia;
14      Vector3    m_torque;
15
16      RigidBody()
17      {
18          // Linear
19          m_position       = Vector3(0,0,0);
20          m_linVelocity    = Vector3(0,0,0);
21          m_invMass        = 0;
22
23          // Angular
24          m_orientation     = Quaternion::Identity();
25          m_angVelocity     = Vector3(0,0,0);
26          m_invLocalInertia = Matrix4::Zero();
27      }//End RigidBody()
28
29      void Integrate(float dt)
30      {
31          // Linear
32          m_linVelocity += m_force * m_invMass * dt; // f=ma
33          m_position    += m_linVelocity * dt;
34          m_force = Vector3(0,0,0);
35
36          // Angular
37          Matrix4 matR = Quaternion::ToRotationMatrix( m_orientation );
38          Matrix4 matT = Matrix4::SetTranslation(m_position);
39          Matrix4 worldInvInertia = Matrix4::Transpose(matR) * ←
            m_invLocalInertia * matR;
40
41          m_angVelocity += Matrix4::Transform( worldInvInertia, m_torque )←
            * dt;
42
43          Quaternion Qvel = (Quaternion(m_angVelocity.x, m_angVelocity.y, ←
            m_angVelocity.z, 0) * 0.5f) * m_orientation;
44          m_orientation += Qvel * dt;
45          m_orientation = Quaternion::Normalize( m_orientation );
46
47          m_torque = Vector3(0,0,0);
48
49      }// End Update(..)
50
51      void AddForce(const Vector3& worldPos, const Vector3& force)
```

```
52    {
53        // Linear
54        m_force += force;
55
56        // Angular
57        m_torque += Vector3::Cross(m_position - worldPos, force);
58
59
60    }// End AddForce(...)
61
62 }; // End class RigidBody
```

Listing 7.3. Example rigid body implementation for 3-dimensions.

7.4 Collisions (Penalty-Springs)

Collision detection returns a boolean type (i.e., 'true' or 'false'). We run collision detection checks for the virtual environment and with other rigid body items. After we have determined a collision we then determine contact information. The contact information is used to calculate 'corrective' forces to counteract the collision. For example, when a rigid body hits the ground, we detect the body has hit the ground, then we determine the contact point, contact normal and penetration depth, which is used to calculate the penalty force.

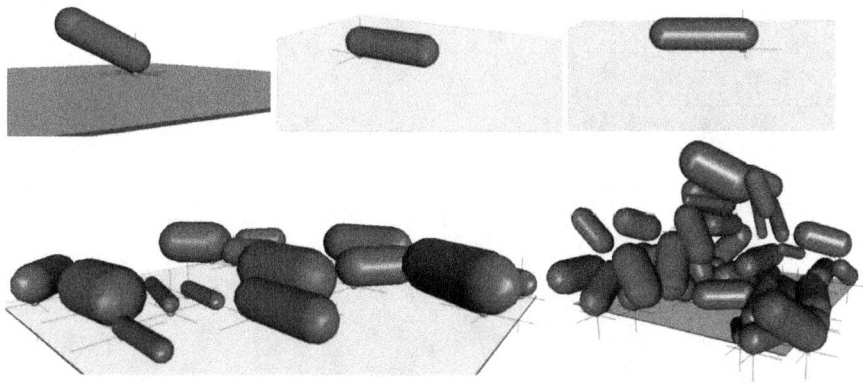

Figure 7.3. *Falling Rigid Bodies* - *Test for a single rigid body and a capsule geometry for collision information. Once the initial penalty forces are working with a single rigid body it is easy to instance large numbers of rigid bodies. (top) single rigid body capsule, (bottom) twenty and sixty rigid body capsules with random lengths and radii.*

7.5 Constraints

Hooke's Law - Constraints (Springs)

$$f_{Hooke} = x\, k_s \tag{7.13}$$

where f_{Hooke} is the Hooke's penalty force, x is the violating distance (i.e., difference between the desired and current length), and k_s is the spring coefficient.

Spring Damping We can add damping into Equation 7.13, as shown below in Equation 7.14:

$$f_{Hooke} = x\, k_s - v\, k_d \tag{7.14}$$

where v is the velocity of the point the constraint is connected to, and k_d is the spring damping coefficient.

```
class RigidBodySpringConstraint
{
private:
// the length between rigidbody rb1 and rb2
// offset in the rest configuration
float restDistance;

// the two rigidbodies that are connected through
// this constraint
RigidBody *rb1, *rb2;

// local offset vector for the attached contact
// on each rigid body
Vector3 local1, local2;

public:

RigidBodySpringConstraint(RigidBody *rb1, const Vector3& ↵
    localOffset1,
            RigidBody *rb2, const Vector3& localOffset2) :
    rb1(rb1), rb2(rb2), local1(localOffset1), local2(localOffset2)
{
    // Make sure both rigid bodies aren't the same
    DBG_ASSERT( rb1 != rb2 );
    // Make sure that both rigid bodies pointers are
    // valid (i.e., not NULL)
    DBG_ASSERT( rb1 != NULL );
    DBG_ASSERT( rb2 != NULL );

    // Calculate the constraint world positions
    // for each rigid body
    Vector3 wpos1 = rb1->GetPos() +
            Matrix4::Transform(rb1->GetRot(), local1);

    Vector3 wpos2 = rb2->GetPos() +
```

```
36              Matrix4::Transform(rb2->GetRot(), local2);
37
38     restDistance = (wpos2 - wpos1).Length();
39
40  }// End RigidBodySpringConstraint(..)
41
42  // This is one of the important methods, where a
43  // single constraint between two rigid bodies rb1 and rb2
44  // is solved the method is called each frame
45  void UpdateConstraint(float dt)
46  {
47      // Typical form:
48      //
49      // F = - ks x - kd v
50      //
51      // where kd is the coefficient of damping and v is the
52      // relative velocity between the two points connected
53      // by the spring. Larger values for kd increase the
54      // amount of damping so the object will come to rest
55      // more quickly.
56      //
57      // For 3D space we represent the typical form as:
58      //
59      // F = -ks (|x|-d)(x/|x|) - kd v
60      //
61      // Where |x| is the distance between the two points
62      // connected to the spring, d is the desired distance
63      // of separation, and x / |x| is the unit length
64      // direction vector between the two points: a to b,
65      // when applying the force to point a and vice versa.
66
67      // More complicated damping is also possible,
68      // including damping proportional to an objects
69      // squared velocity, as well logarithmic functions.
70      // We focus here on simple linear damping.
71
72      // Get the world positions of the two points on the rigid
73      // bodies that our distance constraint is attached
74      Vector3 wpos1 = rb1->GetPos() +
75              Matrix4::Transform(rb1->GetRot(), local1);
76
77      Vector3 wpos2 = rb2->GetPos() +
78              Matrix4::Transform(rb2->GetRot(), local2);
79
80
81      // default spring-damping constants
82      const float khook = 5.0f;
83      const float kdamp = khook*0.0001f;
84
85      // vector from rb1 to rb2
86      Vector3 rb1_to_rb2      = wpos2 - wpos1;
87      // current distance between rb1 and rb2
88      float current_distance   = rb1_to_rb2.Length();
89
90      // # 1 - Compute hook force
91      float   stretchDist = current_distance - rest_distance;
92      Vector3 normal = Vector3::Normalize(rb1_to_rb2);
93      Vector3 fhook  = normal * stretchDist * khook;
94
95      // # 2 - Compute damping force
96      // i.e., damping is opposite to the relative velocity
97      // To incorporate damping into the spring equation,
```

```
98    // we first find the relative velocity between the
99    // two connected rigid bodies 1 and 2 at the
100   // contact points.
101   // We define relative velocity as:
102   Vector3 relvel1 = rb1->GetLinearVelocity() +
103     Vector3::Cross(rb1->GetAngularVelocity(), local1);
104
105   Vector3 relvel2 = rb2->GetLinearVelocity() +
106     Vector3::Cross(rb2->GetAngularVelocity(), local2);
107
108   Vector3 relvel = relvel2 - relvel1;
109
110
111   // We now have the relative velocity of the connecting
112   // points - rigidbody 2 with respect to rigid body 1.
113   // Further, we only want to
114   // dampen motion along the axis of the spring. That
115   // is, we only care about the component of vrel
116   // which lies in the direction of normal. To find this
117   // quantity, we must project the vector vrel onto
118   // normal ; because we have defined normal as a unit
119   // vector, the projection amounts to a dot product.
120   // Our final damping term acting on rigid bodies is:
121
122   float   dampAmount = Vector3::Dot( normal, relvel );
123   Vector3 fdamp     = normal * dampAmount * kdamp;
124
125   // # 3 - Add forces together and apply them to the
126   // rigid bodies:
127   rb1->AddForce( wpos1,  fhook + fdamp );
128   rb2->AddForce( wpos2, -fhook - fdamp );
129
130   }// End UpdateConstraint(..)
131
132
133   // Draw the constraint - i.e. a simple line between
134   // the two rigid bodies
135   void Draw()
136   {
137     // calculate the world position by transforming
138     // the local contact offset
139     Vector3 wpos1 = rb1->GetPos() +
140           Matrix4::Transform(rb1->GetRot(), local1);
141
142     Vector3 wpos2 = rb2->GetPos() +
143           Matrix4::Transform(rb2->GetRot(), local2);
144
145     DrawLine( wpos1, wpos2 );
146   }// End Draw(..)
147
148   }; // End class RigidBodySpringConstraint
```

Listing 7.4. Spring constraint implementation example - for a basic Newtonian rigid body system.

Angular Springs While distance constraints ensure our rigid bodies stay together - within no time at all, our ragdoll bend out of any form of identifiable character form. To ensure our character remains in pose, we add additional 'angular' constraints. Angular constraints work the same as linear constraints, however, we calculate the angular error and apply a correcting torque.

$$\tau_{Hooke} = \theta \ k_s - \omega \ k_d \qquad (7.15)$$

where θ is the error between the current and desired angle, ω is the angular velocity, k_s is the spring coefficient, and k_d is the damping coefficient.

Quaternions and Angular Difference   As we showed in Section 3.7.3, when we discussed angular interpolation using SLERP. We can calculate the angular error in 3-dimensions as an axis-angle - that we can use to apply a corrective torque.

$$q_{err} = q_{cur} \ q^*_{des} \qquad (7.16)$$

where q_{cur} is the current quaternion orientation, q_{des} is the desired quaternion orientation, the '*' indicates the conjugate, which for unit quaternions is the inverse, and q_{err} is the quaternion orientation difference (error). For example, if the current and destination quaternion orientations are the same, the calculation will return a unit quaternion (difference of zero).

7.6 Ragdolls

A ragdoll is made up of interconnected rigid bodies. The rigid bodies represent the limbs (bones) of the character. The motion of the ragdoll is generated through contacts and joint constraint forces. The user can control the ragdoll's motion through external forces (e.g., punch or throw the ragdoll around). In a real-world application, the character would be controlled through kinematic methods (pre-recorded animations), yet when the character is punched, thrown, or dies, the application will switch the character to ragdoll mode. As shown in Figure 7.4, the rigid bodies are connected by distance and angular spring constraints. The distance constraints keep the limbs together, while the angular constraints ensure the character remains in an identifiable pose.

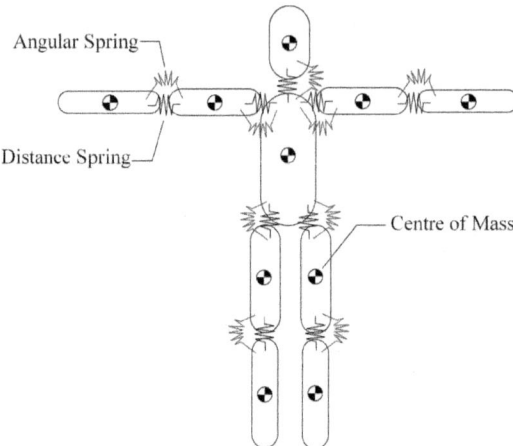

Figure 7.4. *Articulated Ragdoll* - *Character limbs are connected with springs.*

7.7 Procedural (less dependant on data/key-frames)

Procedural content allows us to generate less repetitive content. We can configure and generate huge amounts of data given configuration files. Less dependent on artists to manually create targeted content for every situation. For example, ragdolls are one example of procedural physics-based content that allows the user to interact with the character and is unique to the situation.

- trees
- grass
- particles
- deformations
- scratches/scorch marks
- random character motions (looking around, swaying)
- ...

7.8 Inverse Kinematics (IK)

Inverse kinematics is the opposite of forward kinematics (FK), whereby the end-positions of all the joints are calculated given the joint angles. Inverse kinematics (IK) is a challenging and valuable multi-discipline technique (e.g., animation, graphics, and robotics). The issue inverse kinematics attempts to resolve is to **find a set of joint configurations of an articulated structure based upon the desirable end-effector location.** So for IK we are given the positions of feet and hands and we calculate the articulated character's joint angles to achieve these positions. The topic of IK is vast and beyond the scope of this chapter - however, a simple technique for real-time interactive environments is the cyclic coordinate descent (CCD) algorithm.

$$
\begin{aligned}
\text{forward kinematics:} && x &= f(\theta_0, \theta_1, ..., \theta_n) \\
\text{inverse kinematics:} && [\theta_0, \theta_1, ..., \theta_n] &= f^{-1}(x)
\end{aligned}
\tag{7.17}
$$

As Equation 7.17 shows, the inverse kinematic problem can be highly ambiguous and possess multiple solutions.

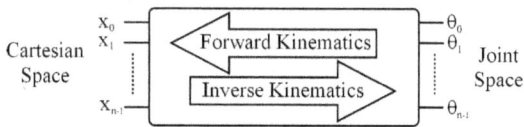

Figure 7.5. *Forward & Inverse Kinematics - Illustrating the relationship between forward and inverse kinematics parameters*

7.8.1 Analytical Inverse Kinematics

The geometric/analytical solution for IK algorithms tend to be very quick because they reduce the IK problem to a single mathematical equation that need only be evaluated once to produce a result (e.g., see Figure 7.6). The limitations of this method becomes apparent in the case of large chains. In such cases, the task of reducing the problem to a single mathematical equation is impractical. Therefore geometric/analytical techniques tend to be less useful in the field of character animation for simple cases (e.g., elbow or knee).

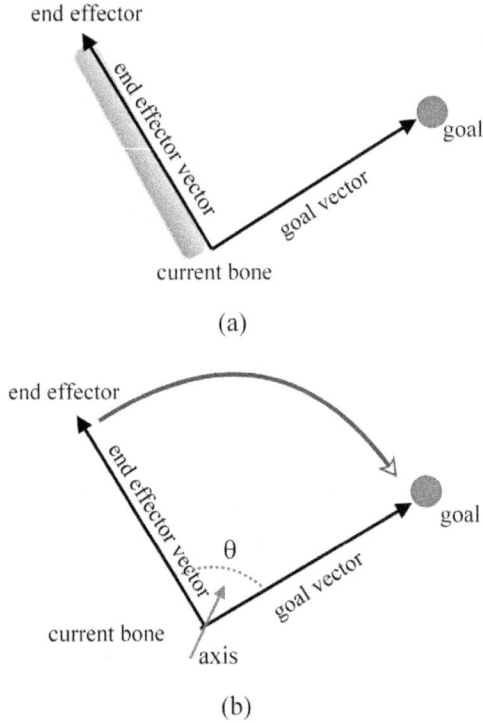

Figure 7.6. *Uncomplicated Analytical Inverse Kinematic Example - Single limb and joint angle (e.g., can be solved using the dot and cross product).*

7.8.2 Cyclic Coordinate Descent (CCD)

IK solvers that are based on CCD use an iterative approach that takes multiple steps towards a solution (see Figure 7.8). CCD works by analysing each joint one-by-one in a progressive refinement philosophy. Starting with the last joint in the chain (e.g., a hand for a character) and orientating it towards the target, then moving down to the next joint and repeating. The steps the method takes is formally defined as a heuristic solution, therefore each step can be performed relatively quickly. An example of a possible heuristic would be to minimise the angle between pairs of vectors created when projecting lines through the current node and end-effector and current node and desired location. However, because the iterative step is heuristically driven, accuracy is normally the price paid for speed. Another issue with this technique is that one joint angle is updated at a time as opposed to the complete hierarchical structure. This has the undesirable and unrealistic result of earlier joints moving much more than later limbs in the IK chain.

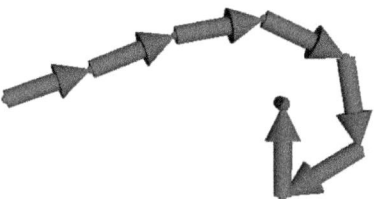

Figure 7.7. *Animated Inverse Kinematic Simulation* - *Real-Time interactive IK simulation screen capture (i.e., following mouse around screen).*

CCD Implementation   The Cyclic Coordinate Descent (CCD) algorithm is an iterative IK solution. The basic idea of the CCD algorithm is to loop over each bone in the IK chain and rotate it such that the end effector (which is typically the last bone in the chain) will move as close as it can to the target position.

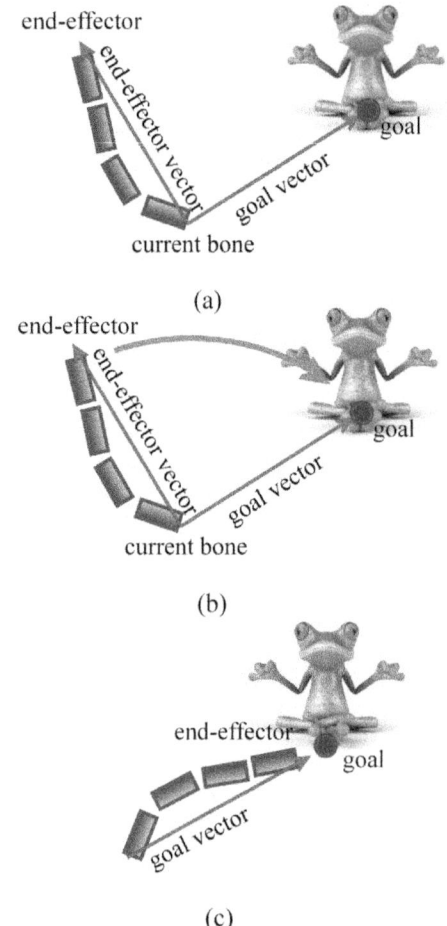

Figure 7.8. *Cyclic Coordinate Descent (CCD)* - *Simple illustration showing the principle of the CCD technique. (a) Compute the vector direction of the current bone to the goal position and the current bone to the end effector; (b) Compute the rotation matrix that will rotate the end effector vector onto the goal vector. To do this, we first compute a rotation axis by taking the cross product of the end effector vector and the goal vector. Next, using the dot product, we calculate the angle between the two vectors. We then compute our rotation matrix using our new axis and angle; (c) Apply the rotation to the current bone.*

Algorithm 2 Algorithm for an IK CCD system - where we start at the final bone in the system and work backwards.

---

  while While distance from effector to target $>$ threshold and numloops<max **do**

    Take current bone

    Build vector V1 from bone pivot to effector

    Build vector V2 from bone pivot to target

    Get the angle between V1 and V2

    Get the rotation direction

    Apply a differential rotation to the current bone

    If at the base node then the new current bone is the last bone in the chain

    Else the new current bone is the previous one in the chain

    EndIf

  end while

7.9 Inverse Dynamics

Inverse dynamics is the process of calculating the necessary forces and torques to achieve a specific change in motion. For example, when we want the articulated character to follow a trajectory specified by an artist - the character is driven by forces and torques but the motion.

$$\text{forward dynamics:} \qquad a = \frac{f}{m}$$
$$\text{inverse dynamics:} \qquad f = m\,a \tag{7.18}$$

where f represents force, m the mass, and a acceleration. The equations of motion can be expanded to include both angular and linear components (i.e., Newton-Euler). However, the concepts are the same, we use matrix based methods to manipulate the problem and solve for either the forces (and torques) or accelerations.

7.10 Summary

We have only scratched the surface of rigid body mechanics, constraints, and collision detection. The principles in this chapter form the foundation - from which you can continue to develop further concepts and algorithms. For example, we have focused on a simple penalty based method, but there are also impulses and constraint based solvers that are better suited for creating more accurate representations.

=

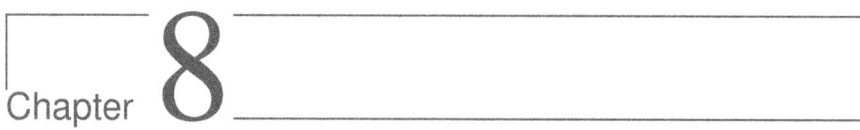

Chapter 8

Deformation (Morphing)

No amount of experimentation can ever prove me right; a single experiment can prove me wrong.

Albert Einstein

8.1 Introduction

We will cover deformation and morphing in this chapter. The deformation (morphing) of an object mesh is simple and straightforward. As shown in Figure 8.1, the mesh is transformed. For morphing situations, the transformation is interpolated between the original and final transform over a specified duration of time. We transform the vertices which results in the edges and faces (in 3-dimensions) and ultimately the visual shape changing.

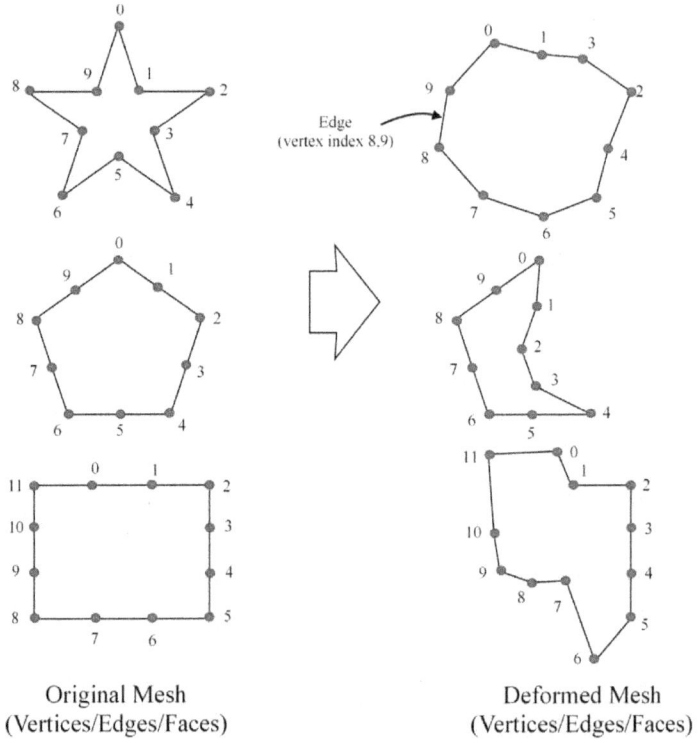

Original Mesh
(Vertices/Edges/Faces)

Deformed Mesh
(Vertices/Edges/Faces)

Figure 8.1. *Deformation/Morphing Concept* - *Original and deformed vertices (transformed) - vertices and edges in 2-dimensions and vertices, edges, and faces in 3-dimensions.*

The deformation or morphing (tweening) of a mesh is the process of changing one shape into another over time. Commonly, the start and end mesh will have the same number of control vertices - however, for multi-resolution systems, we can add or remove additional vertices based upon the fidelity.

- Displacement mapping/height mapping
- Terrain
- Water ripples
- Vehicle dents
- Animation

8.1.1 History

In the past, all animations were achieved using morphing (or tweening), for example, the Quake and Doom animation files, would store arrays of 'key-frames' and interpolate between them to present the visual illusion of movement.

8.1.2 Timing

As explained in Section 3.10, we can relate time with the interpolation. Rather than using an arbitrary float that goes from 0 to 1, we can base the interpolation on the change in time (e.g., how much time has elapsed each frame and how much to interpolate along).

8.2 Global & Local Transforms

We consider two main types of deformation transformations, known as local and global. For local transformations each vertex considers only itself and neighbouring vertices. For world transformations each vertex considers the whole shape (e.g., all vertices, edges, and faces) in the calculations.

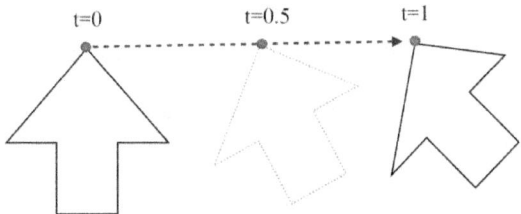

Figure 8.2. *Local Vertex Deformation* - *Going from the source mesh coordinates (scalar value of 0.0), each vertex is gradually moved towards its target mesh coordinates (scalar value of 1.0). The calculation of the coordinates between the star and end position vertex position is easy. For example, 'linear' interpolation calculation is $v(t) = v(0) + (v(1) - v(0))$, where $v(0)$ and $v(1)$ are the start and end locations and t is the scalar value from 0. to 1.0. When $t = 0$ the vertex is at the origin and when $t = 1$ the vertex is at the final location.*

```
1  // vecSource = Vector3 w/source coordinates
2  // vecTarget = Vector3 w/target coordinates
3  // delta     = float   w/scalar value
4
5  // Multiply source coordinates by inversed scalar
6  Vector3 vecSourcePos = vecSource * (1.0f  delta);
7
8  // Multiply target coordinates by scalar
9  Vector3 vecTargetPos = vecTarget * delta;
10
```

```
11  // Add the two resulting vectors together
12  Vector3 vecPos = vecSourcePos + vecTargetPos;
```

Listing 8.1. Example code showing how simple the local interpolation between the start and end vertex location.

8.3 Morphing a Mesh to a Sphere

An uncomplicated practical example to show the transformation of a shape - is to convert an arbitrary mesh to a sphere.

1. Load mesh from a file (e.g., .obj file format).
2. Calculate the final end mesh vertex locations (e.g., project them onto a sphere using the shape centroid).
3. Interpolate between the start and end locations.

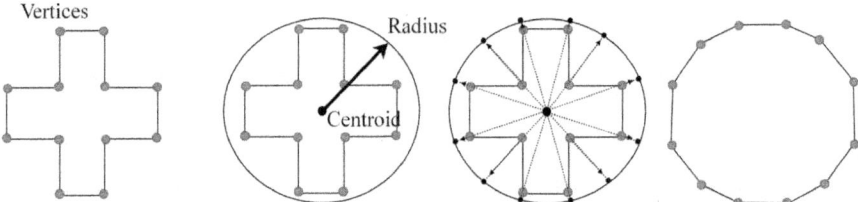

Figure 8.3. *Morphing Example* - *Morphing a simple shape onto a sphere boundary. We calculate the final vertex locations by projecting the starting vertex location through the centroid onto the shapes radius. Once we know the start and end vertex locations we can interpolate between the two shapes over time.*

8.4 Animated Surface Wave (Water)

Displacing a surface height using a trigonometric sine function enables us to create a water like surface (see Figure 8.4). We combine multiple sine waves with varying amplitudes and offsets to create an asthetically pleasing water simulation. Additionally, to have the water 'animate', we include time variable.

$$height = sin(x) + sin(z) \tag{8.1}$$

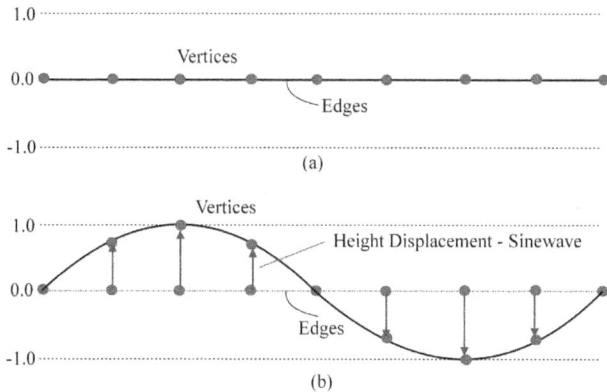

Figure 8.4. *Animated Water Surface* - *Displacing a surface based on a simple trigonometric function, such as, a sine wave, enables us to create a water like surface.*

$$\text{height}_{\text{animated}} = sin(x + time) + sin(z + time) \qquad (8.2)$$

As shown in Figure 8.5, the effect is amplified by adding additional sine waves. Scale the frequency, offset, and amplitude of each sine wave to form a complex ocean-like water effect that ripples analogous to real-world water.

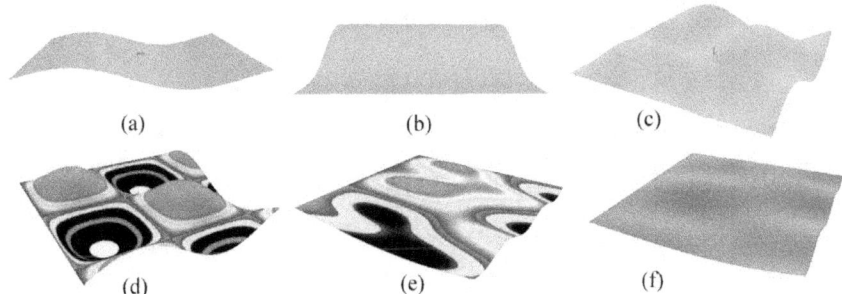

Figure 8.5. *Water Surface* - *(a) single sine wave along the x axis, (b) a single sine wave along the z axis, (c) combined sine wave along both x and z axis, (d) applying a color ramp to the wave height to show visual details, (e) multiple sine waves, and (f) rippling water effect.*

8.5 Kinematics & Physics

The transformation of the shape can be accomplished using simple interpolation methods or using physics-based concepts (i.e., Newton's laws, mass, and velocity). For kinematic methods we consider the start and end locations and interpolate along a trajectory. For physics-based methods we take the start and end locations and use penalty forces to transform the shape coordinates.

Kinematic   For a simple linear kinematics solution, we require three parameters:

p_0 - start position
p_1 - end position
ratio - scalar between 0.0 and 1.0

We calculate the current position as:

$$p(t) = p_0 + (p_1 - p_0)\, ratio \tag{8.3}$$

Physics   For a simple physics-based solution we use a spring-like system requiring five parameters for each point:

p_0 - start position
p_1 - end position
dt - scalar time step in seconds
velocity - vector
mass - scalar
k_s - scalar spring stiffness

The position is maintained using a corrective feedback force proportional to the error, given by:

---

force = $(p_1 - p_0)\, k_s$
acceleration = force / mass   (i.e., Newton's second law - f=m a)
velocity = velocity + acceleration   dt
position = position + velocity   dt

The penalty force is the error between the current and desired particle location.

8.6 Summary

To summarize, the deformation or morphing (tweening) of a mesh is the process of changing one shape into another over time. When we deform or morph a mesh, we gradually change the starting mesh coordinates to another set of coordinates (i.e., a new mesh shape).

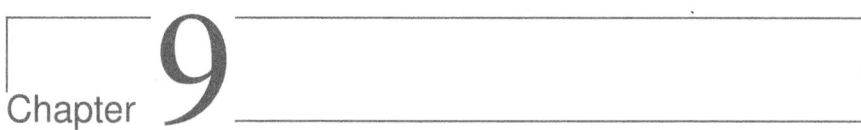

Chapter **9**

Textures and Sprites

You cannot teach a man anything; you can only help him discover it in himself.

Galileo

9.1 Introduction

Texture based methods are one of the oldest approaches for creating animations. The earliest animated films by Disney were all hand drawn; and a textures are essentially an images. Similarly computer games still use animated sprites to create the illusion of movement. In this chapter, we show how textures can be used for more than just sprites. For example, textures can be combined with 3-dimensional geometry, mixed with other textures, or generated using procedural algorithms. Textures in combination with lighting algorithms enable computers to generated scenes that are photo realistic. The textures store more than just decal information, additional data, such as, depth and object velocities. You see this a lot in techniques, like deferred rendering, shadow mapping, and parallel mapping. As textures provide a resource for storing vast amounts of information to create exciting animations. A few examples of texture based animations are:

- Animating Textures (sprites)
- Blurring (diffusing)
- Scrolling
- Water Droplets on a Window
- Blending (mixing multiple textures)
- Indexing (frame sequences)

Texture animation works on a polygon level (by manipulating the image source or texture coordinates a polygon uses) as opposed to working with vertices, as we did in earlier animation techniques mentioned in previous chapters. In this chapter, we present a number of popular texture animation techniques - such as, texture transformations, video media texture animation, and texture-geometry animation.

9.2 Pixels Per Second

Time-based motion does not just apply to 3-dimensional scenes. Movement is also a major part screen based animation. We must guarantee that the motion is consistent, regardless of how fast or how slow our computer is running. A common use for time-based movement is when we want to move an object a set distance over a period of time. For example, suppose the user presses a key to move to the right, so our application or game responds by moving the on-screen object to the right a small amount. Let us say 50 units over a period of one second, which equates to 0.050 units of movement per millisecond. With a small function, we can calculate the number of units (as a floating-point value) to move an object based on the elapsed time between frames:

```
1  float CalculateMovement(float elapsedTime, float pixelsPerSec)
2  {
3    return (pixelsPerSec / elapsedTime);
4  }
```

As we can see in the 'CalculateMovement' function, we are using the following calculation - 'pixelsPerSec / elapsedTime'. The 'pixelsPerSec' variable contains the number of units we want to move over the period of a second. The elapsed time is in seconds. Basically, we're breaking down the number of units to move per second. We need to multiply this by 'elapsedTime' to calculate the total movement. While you may be thinking this sort of time-based motion is very basic, it is, but it should not be overlooked. The knowledge of this time-based movement function is crucial for advanced features, such as, smoothly interpolating images and objects along pre-defined trajectories.

9.3 Fur & Hair

We discuss real-time fur & hair effects using shells - 'with movement'. Texture shells provide a solution for creating a simple real-time dynamic interactive effect (e.g., adding hair/fur effects to 3D models that bounces around). Shells enable us to represent a high level of detailed geometry using low-poly slicing. The complex geometry, i.e., fur and hair in this case, is created using layers, also called shells. Mapping textures onto these shells produces a visual representation of the high detailed model. These textured quads are rendered at relative offsets to the model's surface. The more slices give a more detailed visual representation of the model. This method enables us to create fur effects that run in real-time with high visual detail. We show various enhancements to the basic shell method to generate more exotic, dynamic, and realistic fur effects (e.g., springs and forces).

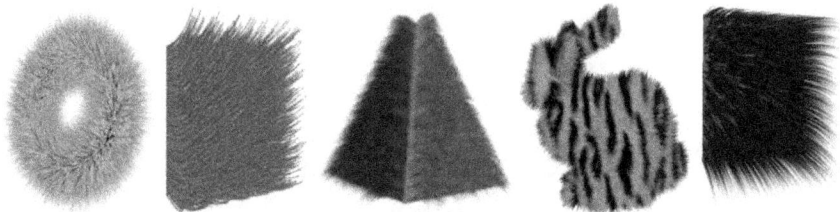

Figure 9.1. *Shell Fur & Hair Effects* - *Projecting multiple instances of the textured surface along the normal to create a computationally efficient and aesthetically pleasing visual fur/hair effect.*

Fur/hair principles A robust and computationally efficient fur & hair effect is indispensable in interactive real-time virtual environments, such as games. A realistic effect that is computationally efficient and straightforward brings an otherwise static and in inflexible scene to life (i.e., objects would follow repetitive motions and wouldn't be interactive).

Dynamic Fur & Hair Shells We can expand the underpinning fur & hair shell principle to encapsulate basic dynamic behaviour by:

- Apply a position-based constraint system to the shell layers to create interactive fur movement (i.e., moves with the model or in response to forces, such as wind)
- Expand the fur & hair effect to create different effects (e.g., thick, think, and long) - e.g., hair that changes over time or grows

Onions The shells are built up like layers on an onion to make up the model. The shells let us achieve high detail objects using a reduced poly model. This method demonstrates excellent real-time results. Starting with a fully transparent texture, noise pixels are scattered across the image, this image is then wrapped across shells which are along the normal of the surface. Varying the number of shells/layers shown in Figure 9.3 demonstrates varying realism using a fixed image. Following on from a constant fixed shell, we alter the shell so that the number of hair pixels is reduced as you move further out towards the outer layers, shown in Figure 9.4. Fur can be combined with texture decal information to create textured fur effects, as shown in Figure 9.1.

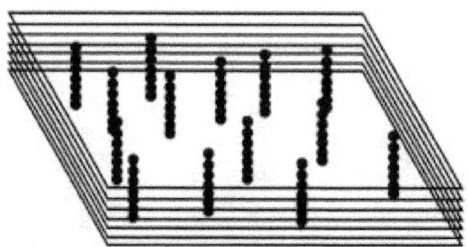

Figure 9.2. *Shell Concept* - *Projecting multiple instances of the textured surface along the normal.*

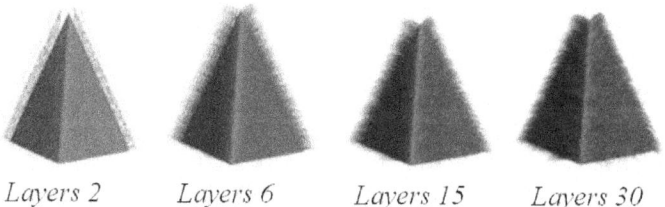

| *Layers 2* | *Layers 6* | *Layers 15* | *Layers 30* |

Figure 9.3. *Shell Numbers* - *Varying the number of shells, offset, and distance apart can create a variety of different effects.*

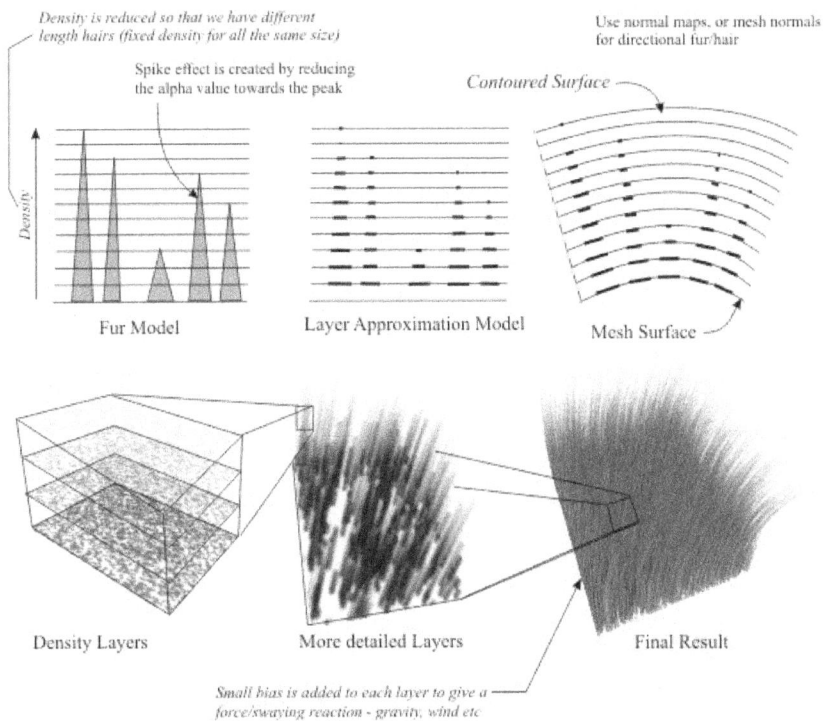

Figure 9.4. *Details* - *Projecting multiple instances of the textured surface along the normal.*

Fur/hair implementation details

1. Takes pre-created image and applies it to a basic shape (i.e., cube)
2. Alpha is enabled and alpha values less than 0 aren't written to the z-buffer
3. Culling is disable to draw the front and the back of the texture (possibly disable for the final effect)
4. Shells are a fixed distance with fixed texture mapped across them

Fur/hair movement with physics   We can expand the basic shell implementation to make it a dynamic fur/hair effect. The tasks is in two parts, modifying the graphical implementation to include additional features (e.g., loading in models and texture/fur patters) and the physics-based part for synthesizing hair motion.

1. Oscillate the layers (e.g., use sin/cosine motion so they gradually oscillate and move)

2. Connect layers together with verlet distance constraints so the hair and fur bounces around as it moves

3. Apply the hair/fur effect to different scenes (e.g., a car or a characters head)

We have introduced an uncomplicated real-time fur & hair simulator for interactive dynamic scenes. Combining basic shells with springs and particles enables us to create an interactive effect suitable for real-time environments, such as games.

9.4 Water Droplets

The water droplet effect is both an image based technique (i.e., to create water ripples on an image) and a geometric effect. For the geometric solution, we take the image and use it to displace the geometry height, as shown below in Figure 9.5. The droplet implementation class is shown in Listing 9.1.

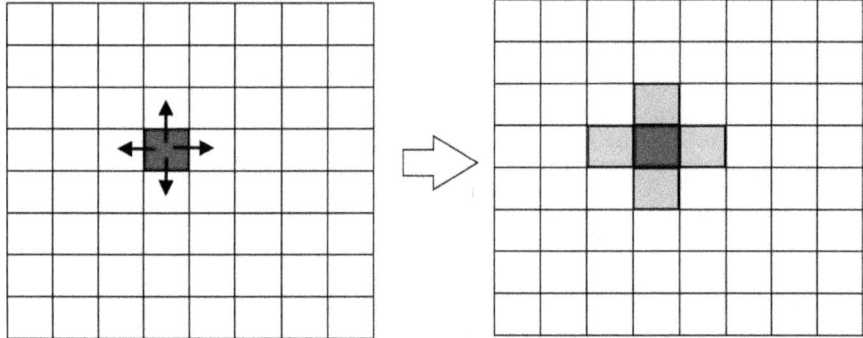

Figure 9.5. *Droplet - Wave amplitude spreads out over the surface.*

```
1
2
3   class WaterDroplet
4   {
5   public:
6   // width/height of our grid
7   int             m_width;
8   int             m_height;
9
10  // two arrays - current and old
11  vector<float>   m_array0;
12  vector<float>   m_array1;
13
14  // reference pointers to swap between two arrays
15  vector<float>*  m_arrayPtrCur;
16  vector<float>*  m_arrayPtrOld;
```

```
17
18   // constructor to resize the arrays
19   WaterDroplet       (int width, int height);
20
21   // Accessors & setters for indexing the array
22   float GetHeight      (const vector<float>& array, int xcoord, int ←
        ycoord);
23   void  SetHeight      (vector<float>& array,      int xcoord, int ←
        ycoord, float val);
24
25   // Update water droplet effect
26   void  UpdateWaveArray ();
27
28   // Insert 'drops' - splashes
29   void  AddDrop        (int xcoord, int ycoord, float val);
30   };
31
32
33   WaterDroplet::WaterDroplet(int width, int height)
34   {
35   m_width  = width;
36   m_height = height;
37   m_array0.resize(width*height);
38   m_array1.resize(width*height);
39   m_arrayPtrCur = &m_array0;
40   m_arrayPtrOld = &m_array1;
41   }// End WaterWaveDropplets()
42
43   // Get and Set accessors to make the code cleaner
44   // and to ensure we don't go out of range with our arrays
45   float WaterDroplet::GetHeight(const vector<float>& array, int xcoord←
        , int ycoord)
46   {
47   // Sanity checks
48   DBG_ASSERT(xcoord>=0 && xcoord<m_width);
49   DBG_ASSERT(ycoord>=0 && ycoord<m_height);
50
51   int index = xcoord + ycoord * m_width;
52   DBG_ASSERT(index>=0 && index<(int)array.size());
53   return array[index];
54   }// End GetHeight(..)
55
56
57   void WaterDroplet::SetHeight(vector<float>& array, int xcoord, int ←
        ycoord, float val)
58   {
59   // Sanity checks
60   DBG_ASSERT(xcoord>=0 && xcoord<m_width);
61   DBG_ASSERT(ycoord>=0 && ycoord<m_height);
62
63   int index = xcoord + ycoord * m_width;
64   DBG_ASSERT(index>=0 && index<(int)array.size());
65   array[index] = val;
66   }// End GetHeight(..)
67
68
69   void WaterDroplet::UpdateWaveArray()
70   {
71   // Debug delay - only update every 10 frames
72   // static int count = 0;
73   // count++;
74   // if ( count%10 != 0 ) return;
```

```
75
76    // This is where the 'waves' are dynamically altered and moved -
77    // and the reason we have two arrays of wave amplitudes (height)
78
79    // Swap old and new arrays
80    vector<float>* tmp   = m_arrayPtrCur;
81    m_arrayPtrCur        = m_arrayPtrOld;
82    m_arrayPtrOld        = tmp;
83
84    // use 3x3 size kernel - however, this could be increased
85    // to create a smoother rippled (e.g., 5x5)
86    for (int i = 1; i < m_width - 1; ++i)
87    {
88    for (int k = 1; k < m_height - 1; ++k)
89    {
90    float height = 0;
91
92    height += GetHeight(*m_arrayPtrOld, i,  k+1); // index directly ↩
          above
93    height += GetHeight(*m_arrayPtrOld, i,  k-1); // index directly ↩
          below
94    height += GetHeight(*m_arrayPtrOld, i+1,k ); // index to the left
95    height += GetHeight(*m_arrayPtrOld, i-1,k ); // index to the right
96
97    height *= 0.45f;
98
99    height -= GetHeight(*m_arrayPtrCur, i  ,k  )*0.8f; // subtract ↩
          previous
100
101   height *= 0.95f;
102
103   SetHeight(*m_arrayPtrCur, i, k, height);
104   }//End inner for loop
105   }// End outer for loop
106
107   }// End UpdateWaveArray(..)
108
109
110   void  WaterDroplet::AddDrop(int xcoord, int ycoord, float val)
111   {
112   SetHeight(*m_arrayPtrCur, xcoord, ycoord, val);
113   }// End AddDrop(..)
```

Listing 9.1. Water droplet sample code.

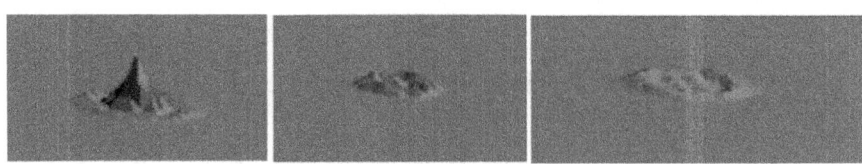

Figure 9.6. ***Water Droplet*** - *Animated plane deformed due to the water droplet wave rippling across the surface.*

9.5 Blur & Velocity

As shown in Chapter 6 and Chapter 7, we can calculate the velocity (rate of change of the position) for drawn pixels on the screen. Each red-green-blue pixel has a velocity scalar associated with it - we use this scalar value to determine which parts of the screen to blur to emphasis a quick moving object. We can apply a blurring kernel (post-processing pass) to the output decal image to add in motion qualities.

9.6 Summary

We have introduced the exciting subject of texture animation. Since a texture is an array of numbers (i.e., a matrix), we are able to exploit image processing methods to go beyond simple sprites, such as, geometry animation, splashes, and fur/hair effects.

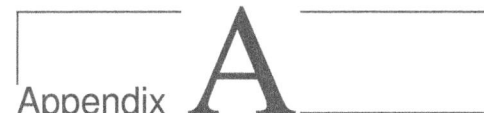

Appendix A

The Appendix

I have not failed. I've just found 10,000 ways that won't work.

Thomas A. Edison

A.1 Asserts

Implementation details for a custom set of assert macros. The macro enables us to catch issues instantly - similarly, the macro can be disabled for final builds or redirected to a log file to help track down difficult problems.

```
1   #ifdef _DEBUG
2   //#define DBG_HALT __asm{ int 3 } // or __debugbreak();
3   #define DBG_HALT { __debugbreak(); }
4   #define DBG_ASSERT(exp) {if ( !(exp) ) {DBG_HALT;}}
5   #define DBG_CHECKFLOAT(f) \
6   {
7   DBG_ASSERT( f!=f ); // NAN
8   DBG_ASSERT( f!=infinity );
9   DBG_ASSERT( f!=-infinity );
10  }
11  #else
12  #define DBG_HALT
13  #define DBG_ASSERT(exp)
14  #define DBG_CHECKFLOAT(f)
15  #endif // _DEBUG
```

A.2 Mathematical Methods

```
1   // Minimal vector class of 3 floats and overloaded math operators
2
3   class Vector3
4   {
5   public:
6   float x, y, z;
7
8   Vector3 (float x, float y, float z) :
9   x(x), y(y), z(z) { };
10
11  Vector3 ()
12  {}
13
14  void  operator+= (const Vector3 &v)
15  {x+=v.x;    y+=v.y;    z+=v.z;}
16  Vector3 operator/  (const float &v)    const
17  {return Vector3(x/v,y/v,z/v);}
18  Vector3 operator-  (const Vector3 &v) const
19  {return Vector3(x-v.x,y-v.y,z-v.z);}
20  Vector3 operator+  (const Vector3 &v) const
21  {return Vector3(x+v.x,y+v.y,z+v.z);}
22  Vector3 operator*  (const float &v)    const
23  {return Vector3(x*v,y*v,z*v);}
24  Vector3 operator-  ()            const
25  {return Vector3(-x,-y,-z);}
26
27  static Vector3  Cross (const Vector3 &vA, const Vector3& vB)
28  {return Vector3(vA.y*vB.z - vA.z*vB.y, vA.z*vB.x - vA.x*vB.z, vA.x*↩
        vB.y - vA.y*vB.x);}
29
30  static float  Dot   (const Vector3 &vA, const Vector3& vB)
31  {return vA.x*vB.x + vA.y*vB.y + vA.z*vB.z;}
32
33  static Vector3 Normalize(const Vector3& v)
34  {
35  const float l = v.Length();
36  return Vector3(v.x/l,v.y/l,v.z/l);
37  }
38
39  float Length()    const         {return sqrt(x*x+y*y+z*z);}
40  float LengthSq()    const         {return (x*x+y*y+z*z);}
41
42  }; // End Vector3(..)
```

```
1   /*
2    * Column-major 4x4 matrix
3    *
4    * Layout:
5    *     0   4   8   12
6    *     1   5   9   13
7    *     2   6  10  14
8    *     3   7  11  15
9    *
10   * 3x3 Rotation Matrix Indices
11   *     0   4   8
12   *     1   5   9
13   *     2   6  10
14   *
```

```
15  *   3x1 Translation Indices
16  *       12
17  *       13
18  *       14
19  *
20  */
21  class Matrix4
22  {
23  public:
24  float m[16];
25
26  Matrix4() { }
27
28  Matrix4(float _00, float _10, float _20, float _30,
29  float _01, float _11, float _21, float _31,
30  float _02, float _12, float _22, float _32,
31  float _03, float _13, float _23, float _33)
32  {
33  m[0]=_00; m[1]=_10; m[2]=_20; m[3]=_30;
34  m[4]=_01; m[5]=_11; m[6]=_21; m[7]=_31;
35  m[8]=_02; m[9]=_12; m[10]=_22;  m[11]=_32;
36  m[12]=_03;  m[13]=_13;  m[14]=_23;  m[15]=_33;
37  }
38
39  float&       operator[]  (int index)     { return m[index]; }
40  const float&  operator[]  (int index) const { return m[index]; }
41
42  static Matrix4 Zero()
43  {
44  static Matrix4 zero(0,0,0,0,0,0,0,0,0,0,0,0,0,0,0,0);
45  return zero;
46  }
47
48  static Matrix4 Identity()
49  {
50  static Matrix4 identity(1, 0, 0, 0, 0, 1, 0, 0, 0, 0, 1, 0, 0, 0, 0,←
          1);
51  return identity;
52  }
53
54  static
55  Matrix4 SetTranslation(const Vector3& t)
56  {
57  Matrix4 mat = Matrix4::Identity();
58  mat.m[12] = t.x;
59  mat.m[13] = t.y;
60  mat.m[14] = t.z;
61  return mat;
62  }
63
64  Vector3 GetTranslation() const
65  {
66  return Vector3(m[12], m[13], m[14]);
67  }
68
69  static Matrix4 SetRotationAxis(const Vector3& axis, float angle)
70  {
71  float s = sin(angle);
72  float c = cos(angle);
73  float t = 1 - c;
74
75  Vector3 ax = Vector3::Normalize( axis );
```

```
76
77   float x = ax.x;
78   float y = ax.y;
79   float z = ax.z;
80
81   Matrix4
82   rotate (t*x*x+c,   t*x*y-s*z, t*x*z+s*y, 0,
83   t*y*x+s*z, t*y*y+c,   t*y*z-s*x, 0,
84   t*z*x-s*y, t*z*y+s*x, t*z*z+c, 0,
85   0,        0,        0,    1 );
86
87   return rotate;
88   }
89
90   static
91   Vector3 Transform(const Matrix4& mat, const Vector3& p)
92   {
93   return Vector3(
94   mat[0]*p.x +
95   mat[4]*p.y +
96   mat[8]*p.z,
97
98   mat[1]*p.x +
99   mat[5]*p.y +
100  mat[9]*p.z,
101
102  mat[2]*p.x +
103  mat[6]*p.y +
104  mat[10]*p.z
105  ) + Vector3( mat[12], mat[13], mat[14] );
106  }
107
108  static
109  Matrix4 Transpose(const Matrix4& mat)
110  {
111  Matrix4 retMat(mat);
112  for(int i = 0; i < 4; i++)
113  { for(int i2 = 0; i2 < 4; i2++)
114  { retMat[i2*4+ i] = mat[i*4+i2]; }
115  } }
116  return retMat;
117  }
118
119  }; // End Matrix4(..)
120
121
122  inline
123  Matrix4 operator*(const Matrix4& lhs, const Matrix4& rhs)
124  {
125  Matrix4 result;
126
127  result[0] = lhs[0]*rhs[0] + lhs[4]*rhs[1] + lhs[8]*rhs[2] + lhs[12]*↵
        rhs[3];
128  result[1] = lhs[1]*rhs[0] + lhs[5]*rhs[1] + lhs[9]*rhs[2] + lhs[13]*↵
        rhs[3];
129  result[2] = lhs[2]*rhs[0] + lhs[6]*rhs[1] + lhs[10]*rhs[2] + lhs↵
        [14]*rhs[3];
130  result[3] = lhs[3]*rhs[0] + lhs[7]*rhs[1] + lhs[11]*rhs[2] + lhs↵
        [15]*rhs[3];
131
132  result[4] = lhs[0]*rhs[4] + lhs[4]*rhs[5] + lhs[8]*rhs[6] + lhs[12]*↵
        rhs[7];
```

```
133    result[5] = lhs[1]*rhs[4] + lhs[5]*rhs[5] + lhs[9]*rhs[6] + lhs[13]*↩
           rhs[7];
134    result[6] = lhs[2]*rhs[4] + lhs[6]*rhs[5] + lhs[10]*rhs[6] + lhs↩
           [14]*rhs[7];
135    result[7] = lhs[3]*rhs[4] + lhs[7]*rhs[5] + lhs[11]*rhs[6] + lhs↩
           [15]*rhs[7];
136
137    result[8] = lhs[0]*rhs[8] + lhs[4]*rhs[9] + lhs[8]*rhs[10] + lhs↩
           [12]*rhs[11];
138    result[9] = lhs[1]*rhs[8] + lhs[5]*rhs[9] + lhs[9]*rhs[10] + lhs↩
           [13]*rhs[11];
139    result[10] = lhs[2]*rhs[8] + lhs[6]*rhs[9] + lhs[10]*rhs[10] + lhs↩
           [14]*rhs[11];
140    result[11] = lhs[3]*rhs[8] + lhs[7]*rhs[9] + lhs[11]*rhs[10] + lhs↩
           [15]*rhs[11];
141
142    result[12] = lhs[0]*rhs[12] + lhs[4]*rhs[13] + lhs[8]*rhs[14] + lhs↩
           [12]*rhs[15];
143    result[13] = lhs[1]*rhs[12] + lhs[5]*rhs[13] + lhs[9]*rhs[14] + lhs↩
           [13]*rhs[15];
144    result[14] = lhs[2]*rhs[12] + lhs[6]*rhs[13] + lhs[10]*rhs[14] + lhs↩
           [14]*rhs[15];
145    result[15] = lhs[3]*rhs[12] + lhs[7]*rhs[13] + lhs[11]*rhs[14] + lhs↩
           [15]*rhs[15];
146
147    return result;
148    }
```

```
1
2      class Quaternion
3      {
4      public:
5      float x, y, z, w;
6
7      Quaternion(float x=0.f, float y=0.f, float z=0.f, float w=1.f): x(x)↩
           , y(y), z(z), w(w) { };
8      Quaternion(const Quaternion& rhs): x(rhs.x), y(rhs.y), z(rhs.z), w(↩
           rhs.w) { };
9
10     Quaternion& operator=(const Quaternion& rhs)
11     {
12     if (this != & rhs)
13     {
14     x = rhs.x;
15     y = rhs.y;
16     z = rhs.z;
17     w = rhs.w;
18     }
19
20     return *this;
21     }
22
23     Quaternion& operator*=(const Quaternion& rhs)
24     {
25     float tmpx = w*rhs.x + x*rhs.w + z*rhs.y - y*rhs.z;
26     float tmpy = w*rhs.y + y*rhs.w + x*rhs.z - z*rhs.x;
27     float tmpz = w*rhs.z + z*rhs.w + y*rhs.x - x*rhs.y;
28     float tmpw = w*rhs.w - x*rhs.x - y*rhs.y - z*rhs.z;
29
30     x = tmpx;
31     y = tmpy;
```

```
32   z = tmpz;
33   w = tmpw;
34
35   return *this;
36   }
37
38   Quaternion& operator+=(const Quaternion& rhs)
39   {
40   w = w+rhs.w;
41   x = x*rhs.x;
42   y = y*rhs.y;
43   z = z*rhs.z;
44   return *this;
45   }
46
47   // convenience function for the identity quaternion
48   static Quaternion Identity()
49   {
50   static Quaternion identity(0, 0, 0, 1);
51   return identity;
52   }
53
54   static
55   Quaternion Conjugate(const Quaternion& q)
56   {
57   return Quaternion(-q.x, -q.y, -q.z, q.w);
58   }
59
60   static
61   float Length(const Quaternion& q)
62   {
63   return sqrt(q.x*q.x + q.y*q.y + q.z*q.z + q.w*q.w);
64   }
65
66   static
67   float LengthSq(const Quaternion& q)
68   {
69   return q.x*q.x + q.y*q.y + q.z*q.z + q.w*q.w;
70   }
71
72   static
73   Quaternion Normalize(const Quaternion& q)
74   {
75   float magInv = 1.f/Length(q);
76
77   return Quaternion(q.x*magInv, q.y*magInv, q.z*magInv, q.w*magInv);
78   }
79
80   static
81   float Dot(const Quaternion& q1, const Quaternion& q2)
82   {
83   return ((q1.x*q2.x) + (q1.y*q2.y) + (q1.z*q2.z) + (q1.w*q2.w));
84   }
85
86   static
87   Quaternion FromAxisAngle(const Vector3& v, float angle)
88   {
89   angle *= 0.5f;
90   float sinAngle = sin(angle);
91
92   Vector3 normVector = Vector3::Normalize(v);
93
94   return Quaternion(normVector.x*sinAngle,
```

```
95    normVector.y*sinAngle,
96    normVector.z*sinAngle,
97    cos(angle));
98  }
99
100   static
101   float ToAxisAngle(const Quaternion& q, Vector3& v)
102   {
103   // The quaternion representing the rotation is
104   //    q = cos(A/2)+sin(A/2)*(x*i+y*j+z*k)
105
106   float sqrLength = q.x*q.x + q.y*q.y + q.z*q.z;
107   if (sqrLength > 0.0f)
108   {
109   float invLength = 1.0f/sqrt(sqrLength);
110
111   v.x = q.x*invLength;
112   v.y = q.y*invLength;
113   v.z = q.z*invLength;
114
115   return 2.f*acos(q.w);
116   }
117   else
118   {
119   // angle is 0 (mod 2*pi), so any axis will do.
120   v.x = 1.0f;
121   v.y = 0.0f;
122   v.z = 0.0f;
123
124   return 0.f;
125   }
126   }
127
128   static
129   Matrix4 ToRotationMatrix(const Quaternion& q)
130   {
131   const float x2 = q.x*q.x;
132   const float y2 = q.y*q.y;
133   const float z2 = q.z*q.z;
134   const float xy = q.x*q.y;
135   const float xz = q.x*q.z;
136   const float yz = q.y*q.z;
137   const float wx = q.w*q.x;
138   const float wy = q.w*q.y;
139   const float wz = q.w*q.z;
140
141   // filling up row-wise
142   Matrix4 mat;
143   mat[0] = 1.0f - 2.0f*(y2+z2);    // [0][0]
144   mat[4] = 2.0f*(xy-wz);           // [0][1]
145   mat[8] = 2.0f*(xz+wy);           // [0][2]
146   mat[12] = 0.f;                   // [0][3]
147
148   mat[1] = 2.0f*(xy+wz);           // [1][0]
149   mat[5] = 1.0f - 2.0f*(x2+z2);    // [1][1]
150   mat[9] = 2.0f*(yz-wx);           // [1][2]
151   mat[13] = 0.f;                   // [1][3]
152
153   mat[2] = 2.0f*(xz-wy);           // [2][0]
154   mat[6] = 2.0f*(yz+wx);           // [2][1]
155   mat[10] = 1.0f - 2.0f*(x2+y2);   // [2][2]
156   mat[14] = 0.f;                   // [2][3]
157
```

```
158    mat[3] = 0.f;              // [3][0]
159    mat[7] = 0.f;              // [3][1]
160    mat[11] = 0.f;              // [3][2]
161    mat[15] = 1.f;              // [3][3]
162
163    mat = Matrix4::Transpose( mat );
164    return mat;
165    }
166
167    static
168    Quaternion FromRotationMatrix(const Matrix4& m)
169    {
170    Quaternion q;
171
172    float trace = m[0] + m[5] + m[10] + 1.f;
173
174    float tolerance = 0.00001f;
175
176    if (trace > tolerance)
177    {
178    float root = sqrt(trace);
179    q.w = 0.5f*root;
180    root = 0.5f/root;
181    q.x = (m[6]-m[9]) * root;
182    q.y = (m[8]-m[2]) * root;
183    q.z = (m[1]-m[4]) * root;
184    }
185    else
186    {
187    if (m[0] > m[5] && m[0] > m[10])
188    {
189    float root = sqrt(m[0] - m[5] - m[10] + 1.f);
190    q.x = 0.5f*root;
191    root = 0.5f/root;
192    q.y = (m[1]-m[4]) * root;
193    q.z = (m[8]-m[2]) * root;
194    q.w = (m[6]-m[9]) * root;
195    }
196    else if (m[5] > m[10])
197    {
198    float root = sqrt(m[5] - m[0] - m[10] + 1.f);
199    q.y = 0.5f*root;
200    root = 0.5f/root;
201    q.x = (m[1]-m[4]) * root;
202    q.z = (m[6]-m[9]) * root;
203    q.w = (m[8]-m[2]) * root;
204    }
205    else
206    {
207    float root = sqrt(m[10] - m[0] - m[5] + 1.f);
208    q.z = 0.5f*root;
209    root = 0.5f/root;
210    q.x = (m[8]-m[2]) * root;
211    q.y = (m[6]-m[9]) * root;
212    q.w = (m[1]-m[4]) * root;
213    }
214    }
215
216    return q;
217    }
218
219    static
```

```
220   Quaternion Slerp(float t, const Quaternion& p, const Quaternion& q)
221   {
222   Quaternion ret;
223
224   float cs = Quaternion::Dot(p, q);
225   float angle = acos(cs);
226
227   if (abs(angle) > 0.0f)
228   {
229   float sn = sin(angle);
230   float invSn = 1.0f/sn;
231   float tAngle = t*angle;
232   float coeff0 = sin(angle - tAngle)*invSn;
233   float coeff1 = sin(tAngle)*invSn;
234
235   ret.x = coeff0*p.x + coeff1*q.x;
236   ret.y = coeff0*p.y + coeff1*q.y;
237   ret.z = coeff0*p.z + coeff1*q.z;
238   ret.w = coeff0*p.w + coeff1*q.w;
239   }
240   else
241   {
242   ret.x = p.x;
243   ret.y = p.y;
244   ret.z = p.z;
245   ret.w = p.w;
246   }
247
248   return ret;
249   }
250
251   }; // End Quaternion(...)
252
253
254   inline
255   Quaternion operator*(const Quaternion& q1, const Quaternion& q2)
256   {
257   return Quaternion(q1.w*q2.x + q1.x*q2.w + q1.y*q2.z - q1.z*q2.y,
258   q1.w*q2.y + q1.y*q2.w + q1.z*q2.x - q1.x*q2.z,
259   q1.w*q2.z + q1.z*q2.w + q1.x*q2.y - q1.y*q2.x,
260   q1.w*q2.w - q1.x*q2.x - q1.y*q2.y - q1.z*q2.z);
261   }
262
263   inline
264   Quaternion operator+(const Quaternion& q1, const Quaternion& q2)
265   {
266   return Quaternion(q1.x+q2.x,
267   q1.y+q2.y,
268   q1.z+q2.z,
269   q1.w+q2.w);
270   }
```

Index

Index